WATERSIDE
In Essex

Ann and Norman Skinner

COUNTRYSIDE BOOKS
NEWBURY, BERKSHIRE

First published 1999
© Ann and Norman Skinner 1999

COUNTRYSIDE BOOKS
3 Catherine Road
Newbury, Berkshire

ISBN 1 85306 565 X

Designed by Graham Whiteman
Cover illustration by Colin Doggett
Maps and photographs by Ann Skinner

Produced through MRM Associates Ltd., Reading
Printed by Woolnough Bookbinding Ltd., Irthlingborough

Contents

AREA MAP SHOWING LOCATIONS OF THE WALKS

Walk

❧❀❧

PUBLISHER'S NOTE

We hope that you obtain considerable enjoyment from this book; great care has been taken in its preparation. Although at the time of publication all routes followed public rights of way or permitted paths, diversion orders can be made and permissions withdrawn.

We cannot of course be held responsible for such diversion orders and any inaccuracies in the text which result from these or any changes to the routes nor any damage which might result from walkers trespassing on private property. We are anxious though that all details covering the walks are kept up to date and would therefore welcome information from readers which would be relevant to future editions.

INTRODUCTION

Walking near water has a curiously satisfying effect. These walks along the waterways of Essex are spaced throughout the county (though obviously many are to the south and east where water is in abundance!) and we visit all the major rivers, from the mighty Thames where it is wide and strong just 22 miles from the point where it meets the ocean, to the little River Roding.

In the west of the county, there is a delightful walk by the River Ching in Epping Forest, where the trees are at their best in spring growth or with the golden tints of autumn, and another by the bird hides of the Lee Navigation and Old River Lea, while further north along our border with Hertfordshire walks follow the River Stort – and such a vast collection of things to see, from water meadows and nature reserves to canal locks, boats and an abundance of wild life. The River Roding is crossed by the Tun bridge at a very pretty spot near High Ongar, while the Chelmer enhances a visit to Thaxted, one of the loveliest towns in Essex with its famous church and windmill. Nearer to our county town, a walk from Writtle follows the Can and the Wid before they both join the Chelmer. The Colne is met twice, once beneath the awesome railway viaduct that spans the valley at Chappel and again at the little crossing at Ford Street. To the east of the county, there are walks to follow the Blackwater and the Thames, the Stour, the Crouch and the Colne as they meet the sea. This is not to forget the canals, and the flooded gravel pits that attract so much birdlife, the creeks so beloved of sailors, and the salt marshes that stretch out wild to the sea!

Lovers of birdwatching will find much to occupy them on these walks, but there are wonderful views too and a great deal to appeal to anyone interested in the history of Essex – Tilbury's restored fort, St Cedd's little chapel, the elegant grandeur of St Osyth's priory, smugglers' haunts, blacksmiths' forges and ancient churches, to name but a few.

Please remember that in wet seasons the paths on canal banks and sea walls can sometimes be soft and muddy so suitable footwear is advisable, as is having a small bag with you containing rainwear or a drink if they might be needed during the walk. A clean pair of shoes in the car for when you visit the pubs and other places of interest might be a good idea too. Really good times for these waterside walks are warm dry days in summer and crisp dry days in winter – but you will find enjoyment whatever the weather! Anyway, we are fortunate in Essex in having the driest climate in the country, so these cautionary remarks are probably less needed than you might think!

For your extra enjoyment, each walk has suggestions for places to eat and drink, either on the route or nearby, and telephone numbers so that you can check opening times or menus if you wish. Parking places are given, but if you have to park on the roadside please respect the local residents and the environment. Places of interest nearby are also suggested, if you want to extend your walk into a day out.

The walks are accompanied by a sketch map and the relevant Ordnance Survey map in the Landranger series is given if you would like to follow the route in more detail. The walks, which are all circular, range in length from 2½ to 6½ miles.

We would like to thank our sailing friends for information about the special villages and watersides they know and love. It is always a pleasure when we find that our readers gain so much from visiting the countryside, especially as many of them have not previously been regular walkers. We hope that you will find here places you have never visited before, and we wish you every possible enjoyment on your walks.

Ann and Norman Skinner

THE WATERS OF EPPING FOREST

A lovely stroll through a small corner of Epping Forest, tracing the little River Ching back to the beautiful expanse of Connaught Water. Forest paths and pools, Chingford Plain and picturesque old buildings make this walk a delight.

Butlers Retreat

Epping Forest was claimed for the people by Act of Parliament in 1878 and opened by Queen Victoria in 1882 – 'dedicated to the delectation of the public for ever'. And delectable it is, all 6,000 acres or so of it. It's not surprising that a day out in Epping Forest has been enjoyed by so many. The walk starts opposite the magnificent Royal Forest Hotel, the venue for many a Londoner's outing over the past century, and passes Warren Pond before reaching the River Ching. Despite its grand sounding name it is a mere four to five feet wide here, flowing south to meet the River Lea. Follow it northwards through the forest to beautiful Connaught Water, named after the Duke of Connaught, the very first

Ranger of the Forest appointed by Queen Victoria. You arrive back at Butlers Retreat, which has been providing refreshments for Forest visitors for many decades. Nearby is the picturesque timber-framed Queen Elizabeth's Hunting Lodge, more recently used as a Forest museum but built originally for Henry VIII. It was a kind of grandstand for those who wanted to follow the progress of the royal chase when this was a hunting forest – it is said that once Queen Elizabeth rode her horse up the wooden stairs to the viewing platform on top.

Butlers Retreat has a fine restaurant, with a menu outside the door so you can make a choice before you go in. If you ring direct they will give you details of their menu choices and take reservations on 0181 524 2976. The Royal Forest Hotel is a family pub in the Brewers Fayre chain. They have in their pub/restaurant a choice of four cask ales plus the full range of normal pub drinks. The menu includes a wide range of meals from salmon to steak and kidney pie to steaks. Sandwiches and baps are also available for those wanting a 'lite bite'. Telephone 0181 523 7246.

- **HOW TO GET THERE:** From junction 26 on the M25 take the signs for Epping. At the top of the hill about 2 miles from the junction you come to the Wake Arms roundabout. Take the A104 south-west. After about 4 miles turn right onto the A1069 signed Chingford and look for a parking sign on your left after about 1 mile.

  By train, go to Chingford Station then walk down Station Road and just beyond Bury Road on the left, go half-left across the green uphill to the Royal Forest Hotel.

- **PARKING:** In the public car park signed Epping Forest Museum Car Park. This is opposite the Royal Forest Hotel and Queen Elizabeth Hunting Lodge.

- **LENGTH OF THE WALK:** 2½ miles. Maps: OS Landranger 166 Luton and Hertford, 167 Chelmsford, Harlow and surrounding area (GR 397947).

THE WALK

1. Take the track opposite the Royal Forest Hotel towards Warren Pond. When you reach the pond walk to the right of it. Just before a gate turn left, still keeping beside the pond. When you come to the far end of the pond stay on the bridleway. You will find this swings left then right, marked with a white post and a horseshoe. You soon come to an open space, cross this to a white post straight ahead. Ignore the track and post on your left. Cross a wide bridge over the River Ching.

9

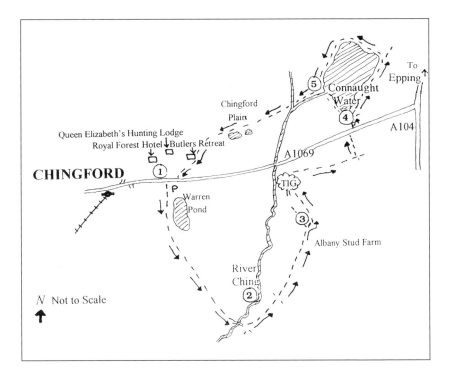

2. Turn left along the wide grass track. The River Ching is on your left now, hidden by brambles. Keep on this bridleway ignoring tempting crossing tracks, epecially where some muddy bits appear. White posts with a horseshoe painted on them guide you as the river becomes close again. Soon horse paddocks appear on your right over the hedge in Albany Stud Farm.

3. As the bridleway goes left, keep near the fence on your right. Take the small path on your right to the holly bushes. This brings you directly beside the fence. In a few yards this path turns left to go over a narrow ditch to a wide clearing. Head slightly left to pass an oak tree with 'TIG' painted in yellow. Cars can be seen on the road ahead as you cross the clearing. Take the track on your right just before the road; it is again marked with a horseshoe. Walk on for about ¼ mile. At a crossing track turn left on a broad green path towards the road and the parked cars. Cross the road with care and walk through the car park to the edge of Connaught Water.

4. Turn right and walk up the right bank of the lake. You will soon come to the remnants of the quay for the long-closed rowing boat station. You will often find children and their parents here with handfuls of bread for the many birds that live on the lake. You may wish to take supplies with you and join in the fun! At the end of the water cross the bridge on your left and keep on round the lake. You will see several small islands with trees out in the lake. When we walked round the birds seemed to be having a high old time, swimming and flying between the islands and the shore. There are seats scattered round the edge of the lake for those who want to have a rest or just sit and enjoy the scene.

5. Continue round the shore till you come to a wire grating over the edge of the lake. Turn right here downhill with the River Ching on your left. Cross a slatted wooden bridge ahead. The path ahead is over the edge of the Chingford Plain and so is relatively open. You cross a bridleway and follow a broad green track uphill and very slightly left. Pass Butlers Pond on your left. When you reach Butlers Retreat, at the rear you will find a fountain. It was a gift of Sir Edwin During Lawrence Burt MP in 1899. It no doubt provided many a thirsty visitor (and their horse) with a welcome drink of water. Walk past the left of the Retreat building and cross the road back to your car, taking time perhaps to have a look at Queen Elizabeth's Hunting Lodge before you leave.

PLACES OF INTEREST NEARBY

The Queen Elizabeth Hunting Lodge is open from 2 pm to 5 pm Wednesday to Sunday. For more information ring the *Epping Forest Information Centre* on 0181 508 0028. The Centre at High Beech (off the A104 from the Robin Hood roundabout) provides information and displays about the Forest. It also houses a gift shop where you can buy local maps and guides. It is open from April to October, Monday to Saturday 10 am to 5 pm; Sunday and bank holidays 11 am to 5 pm. From November to March restricted opening hours apply.

A KING'S WEIR AT FISHERS GREEN

Abundant birdlife and lovely views enhance this walk in the Lee Valley, following the Lee Navigation and the Old River Lea. There is a reminder of the Great Fire of London, and a very pretty weir to enjoy.

The River Lee Navigation

This beautiful area of flooded old sand and gravel pits lying alongside a canal, a river and a large flood relief channel with its variety of birds, insects and plants is a place to be enjoyed by those who love the great outdoors. It has been designated a site of special scientific interest. You can visit two bird hides (normally open free of charge on weekends and bank holidays but to check telephone 01992 702200) and there are seats where you can sit and enjoy the abundance of birdlife along the twisting banks of the Old River Lea. When you climb uphill to enjoy the views, you will also find an old coal post. There were once 219 Coal Duty Posts marking the crossing of the City's Coal Tax boundary. They formed a ring of iron around London with no lane or byway forgotten, and denoted the collection point for taxes imposed by the City of London after the Great Fire in 1666, for the rebuilding work. There has long been a history of market gardening in the Lee Valley and along your way you will pass a nursery specialising in growing English peppers! On your way back, you pass the fascinating Kiora Radial Gates and the very pretty King's Weir.

Those wanting a prepared meal will find a warm welcome at the Coach and Horses about 2 miles north-east from Fishers Green on the B194. They have a range of bitters on hand pump plus all the normal drinks. A blackboard menu offers well priced choices like mouth-watering steak and kidney pie and curries plus a range of ploughman's and sandwiches. They also have a full pudding menu if you want to be really naughty.

Telephone 01992 893151.

- **HOW TO GET THERE:** Fishers Green is between Waltham Abbey and Broxbourne. Those coming from north, east or central Essex should make for southern Harlow leaving on the A1169. Now follow the signs for Broadley Green, then Nazeing. Keep straight on at the roundabout after the King Harold's Head pub to pass the Coach and Horses. You are now on the B194. In 2 miles turn right, marked Hayes Hill and Holyfield Hall Farms, to Lee Valley Park. In about 50 yards turn left on a park road that takes you over several sleeping policemen to the woodland car park. From Waltham Abbey, follow the B194 north and look on the left for the Lee Valley sign. It is the road *after* Fishers Green Lane.
- **PARKING:** There is free parking on the right of the road you have just come in on. The entrance is near the toilet block. There is a tourist information board here to help you find out more about the area.
- **LENGTH OF THE WALK:** 4½ miles. Map: OS Landranger 166 Luton and Hertford (GR 377033).

THE WALK

1. From the car park follow the direction on the wooden sign outside the toilet block, Broxbourne (west). After 50 yards turn right and walk through the kissing gate. The path takes you through a picnic area with the flood relief channel on your left. Pass a car park on your right. Continue on this path till you come to the sign 'Follow path round field'. This takes you out onto the sailing club road. At the road turn left. You will pass several yellow arrows marked Lee Valley link. Just

13

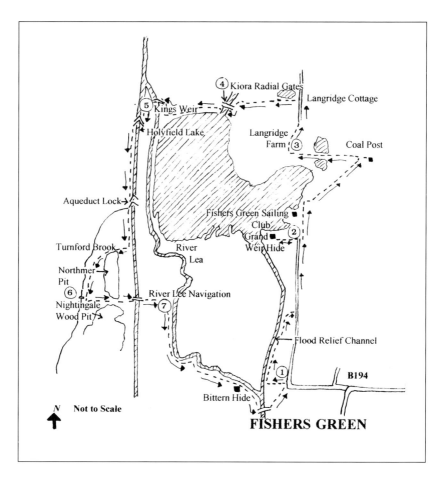

4 Kiora Radial Gates
Langridge Cottage
5 Kings Weir
Holyfield Lake
Langridge Farm 3
Coal Post
Aqueduct Lock
Fishers Green Sailing Club 2
Grand Weir Hide
Turnford Brook
River Lea
Northmer Pit
6
Nightingale Wood Pit
River Lee Navigation
7
Flood Relief Channel
1
B194
Bittern Hide
N Not to Scale
FISHERS GREEN

before Fishers Green Sailing Club you will notice a red path on your left. Take this for a visit to Grand Weir Hide. Retrace your steps to the sailing club and cross over the road to the stile opposite.

2. Having crossed the stile, turn left to continue with the hedge and the sailing club on your left. At the end of the field the yellow arrow indicates your path is right with the hedge on your left. Cross a stile by an oak tree and climb the hill to signposts at the top. Take a rest – and a look at the view if you have not been doing this several times already on your way up! When refreshed turn left over the bridge and then right for about ten paces to view the coal post. Retrace your steps, passing the bridge to go under a five-foot wooden bar. Descend with an orchard

King's Weir

on your right till you come to a yellow waymark on a post. Turn right to cross the scrub ground and join a track that runs past the western edge of the orchard then left to the next yellow waymark. Your route is between the two large earth mounds and onto a high track between two gravel pits, heading for Langridge Farm.

3. You walk turning right between the farm buildings and the house, coming out onto the farm road. You then walk past the nurseries where they grow the English peppers. Just after Langridge Cottage turn left over a wooden bridge with a pit lake on your right. Walk the length of this fishery path then turn left with a fence on your right to join the main footpath. Turn right on the footpath, in a few steps the yellow arrow confirms you are on the correct route. Walk past another arrow onto open scrub land, and head for a sign 'Caution site traffic'. Cross the site road half-right to a yellow upright footpath marker, then go left to walk with the Kiora Radial Gates wire fence on your right. The Gates are named after the Kiora cafe that used to stand near here; Kiora being the brand name of a soft drink popular at the time.

4. Turn right, then left up the steps and over the bridge. At the end of the bridge go down the steps and half-left over an earth bridge. You continue in this direction through a small wooden gate and walk with Holyfield Lake on your left till you enter the wooded path with metal kissing gate and bridge. More metal railings lead you left and right on a long metal bridge over King's Weir. Through more metal railings you reach the River Lee Navigation.

5. Turn left and walk past King's Weir house. Cross the navigation on a concrete bridge and turn left to walk with the navigation on your left. Walk along passing Aqueduct Lock till in ¼ mile you come to a sign 'Turnford Brook 900m'. Turn right here and walk round Northmer Pit with the pit on the left and later Turnford Brook on your right. You pass a pit viewpoint on a wooden bridge, a good place for another rest. Or maybe you prefer the benches further on, also a good place from which to watch the birds.

6. As a wooden bridge appears on the right the yellow track becomes a grey path. At this point turn left, the sign says 'Fishers Green 600m'. Walk between Northmer Pit on your left and Nightingale Wood Pit on your right, then cross the high bridge ahead. You are crossing the River Lee Navigation.

7. After 100 yards the tracks divide. Both lead to the car park but the prettier walk is to turn right and walk with the Old River Lea on your left. You soon come to Bittern Hide on your right. The next green bridge on your left crosses the river. Walk ahead with picnic benches on your left back to the road and the car.

PLACES OF INTEREST NEARBY
Waltham Abbey and the *Lee Valley Park Information Centre* are not far. Go south from Fishers Green and follow the brown signs. Telephone 01992 702200.

ALONG THE STORT FROM ROYDON

The River Stort and Stort Navigation provide the setting for a peaceful country walk from Roydon village along field paths and colourful riverbanks, with canal locks and a traditional hay meadow and nature reserve providing added interest.

Hunsdon Mill Lock

The delightful village of Roydon has houses both ancient and modern, four pubs, a church with an intriguing font, and a village green. The Church House is said to have been built in 1475. Your walk takes you over the little Canons Brook towards the River Stort, and for a lovely stroll along the river bank with flowering shrubs cascading down to the very water's edge. Beautiful Hunsdon Mill Lock marks the junction of the river and the Stort Navigation, which you follow back to Roydon. Hunsdon Mead Nature Reserve is a 60 acre hay meadow rich in wildflowers, managed on the ancient Lammas system – the grass is allowed to grow undisturbed till the end of July, then cattle are grazed there. Lammas Day was traditionally the 1st of August, and grazing can continue until the end of February. The reserve is managed by the Essex Wildlife Trust and you can get more information from the centre at Fingringhoe (telephone 01206 729678).

Two local pubs, both of which serve excellent food are on your route. The White Hart is a pub that prides itself on its range of traditional English food. You can get anything here from sandwiches through hot baguettes to a four course meal in their restaurant. The extended menu includes steaks and Thai cooking. They carry Marsden bitters and Banks real ale as well as the full range of drinks including lager and cider. For more information or to book in the restaurant telephone 01279 792118. The Crusader is just across the road. It carries McMullens bitters, Fosters lager and the full range of drinks including cider. The blackboard menu, changed daily, includes dishes like fish and chips and chicken chasseur. They also serve a range of balti and other curries. Telephone 01279 792161.

- **HOW TO GET THERE:** Take the B181 from Epping to Roydon if coming from the south or east. From the north take the A1169 from Harlow then follow the signs via Eastend to Roydon.
- **PARKING:** There is a public car park in the centre of Roydon. Opposite the White Horse turn into Beaumont Park Drive and about 100 yards up on the right you will find the entrance to the car park.
- **LENGTH OF THE WALK:** 4½ miles. Map: OS Landranger 167 Chelmsford, Harlow and surrounding area (GR 410099).

THE WALK

1. Leave the car park and walk past the White Horse pub. Turn right downhill passing the White Hart, the Crusader and the New Inn. At the war memorial turn right along the side of the village green, then almost immediately right again at a footpath sign beside St Peter's Cottage. Go through the kissing gate and along the twitten (passageway) to the next kissing gate.

2. As you enter this large meadow keep the old hedge on your right. At the stream go ahead over the bridge and stile to the hedged path at the rear of gardens on your left. At the end of the gardens turn left at a yellow waymark post and walk down the side of the last garden till you reach the stream before the railway lines. Turn right and walk with the railway on your left till you come to a track joining from your right.

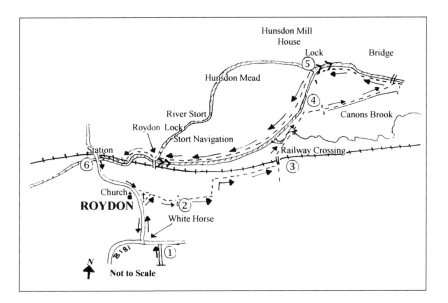

3. On your left you will see the railway crossing – a stile, wooden crossing sleepers and a second stile. Cross with care. Continue in the direction indicated by the yellow arrow on the stile. You are heading to the right of a finger of water and for the rails of the bridge that is clearly visible slightly to your right. Cross the bridge over Canons Brook, noting the signs that indicate you are entering an area to which the Countryside Stewardship Scheme has been applied and you can walk anywhere in the area shown on their map. You continue ahead to the edge of the Stort Navigation. Sometimes this area can get a little boggy so circle round the puddles if necessary.

4. After 100 yards turn right along the field edge keeping the ancient hedgerow on your right. As the high bridge comes into close view the path makes a straight line for it. When the bridge over the river is reached turn left along its southerly bank. This next section is our favourite part of the walk. Cross over a wooden bridge, then a concrete bridge, along the riverside to Hunsdon Mill Lock and House. A perfect place for an apple stop if you have brought supplies with you. Just before you reached the lock you will have spotted that the river and the navigation divide and the river runs off to the right in a big loop. When you reach a white painted gate at the end of the lock, turn right and cross the River Stort Navigation.

Roydon village

5. Turn left and walk to the stile. Across this on your right is the hay meadow of Hunsdon Mead Nature Reserve. From the stile keep on the old towing path with the nature reserve on your right and walk the navigation passing Roydon Lock. Leave the lock by the gate with the yellow waymark on your right and walk the watery loop round to the right. You now go via the kissing gate to pass under the railway line along to the station.

6. When you reach the station turn left to cross the old stone bridge and walk up Roydon High Street. With time on your hands you may wish to look at the 750 year old church, and perhaps like us you might fall in love with the Church House which stands just in front. On the green the village sign reminds us Roydon was recorded in the Domesday book in 1086. When you are ready, retrace your steps to the car.

PLACES OF INTEREST NEARBY

The Ada Cole Rescue Stables at Broadley Green is a lovely place to bring children on a visit. A horse sanctuary where horses are cared for in a safe environment, it is open to the public from 2 pm to 5 pm. There is an entrance charge for adults. Telephone 01992 892133.

FROM SPELLBROOK LOCK TO LITTLE HALLINGBURY

This pretty walk on the Hertfordshire-Essex border takes you along the tow path of the Lee-Stort Navigation and then uphill to the village of Little Hallingbury and lovely views across the valley.

Approaching Tednambury Lock

The River Stort, here also the Lee-Stort Navigation, rises in the north-west of the county and meanders along the border with Hertfordshire, sometimes one side, sometimes the other. Here at Little Hallingbury the walk route is along its well kept tow path, from Spellbrook Lock. Tednambury Lock can sometimes be a hive of activity – on the day I went this way there was a barge going through, cows crossing the farm bridge, and walkers on the tow path! Twyford Bury Lock is a favourite place for canoeists on a fine day. Little Hallingbury is a lovely village with a Norman church. The 'bury' of the name comes from the Iron

Age hill fort above Spellbrook Lock, obviously a fine defensive site. Little Hallingbury Mill marks your way inland to climb the hill to Gaston Green, and superb views of the valley below.

The Three Horse Shoes pub in Spellbrook is now a huge family eating house with the normal range of children's and adults' meals always available though it does tend to get very busy at weekends. The Sutton Arms on the Little Hallingbury to Hatfield Heath road (A1060) is another good choice: telephone 01279 730460 for menu suggestions. Or the Cock at Hatfield Broad Oak can be recommended. The food here is excellent and they carry a wide range of real ales. Telephone 01279 718306.

- **HOW TO GET THERE:** Take the A1060 out of Hatfield Heath north-west towards Little Hallingbury. The route takes you under the M11. About 1 mile further turn left opposite the George pub into Dell Lane. It is signposted Spellbrook.
- **PARKING:** Parking is available in a lay-by on your left as you go down the hill before the lock. Or over the canal and railway in another larger lay-by outside the Three Horse Shoes pub.
- **LENGTH OF THE WALK:** 4¼ miles. Map: OS Landranger 167 Chelmsford, Harlow and surrounding area (first lay-by GR 492176, second lay-by GR 488175).

THE WALK

1. Walk on along the road if you are at the first lay-by, to Spellbrook Lock. From the lay-by outside the pub, walk back over the level crossing (note the change of spelling on the manned level crossing – Spelbrook) and over the River Stort water management channel to Spellbrook Lock. At footpath sign No 38 turn south to walk the tow path with the canal on your right. The tow path will take you through a white gate into a private fishery. At the river bend cross the bridge into Sawbridgeworth Angling Society Area.

2. Round the next bend you come to Tednambury Lock and this is where you leave the navigation. Turn left almost back on yourself when you are level with the cattle bridge at the far end of the lock. You will pick up a faint track running north-east. There is a pole and wire fence 20 paces to your right, and the path you are following goes through the second opening in the fence about 20 paces after a tree with a big Private Fishing sign. Head half-left to the white buildings.

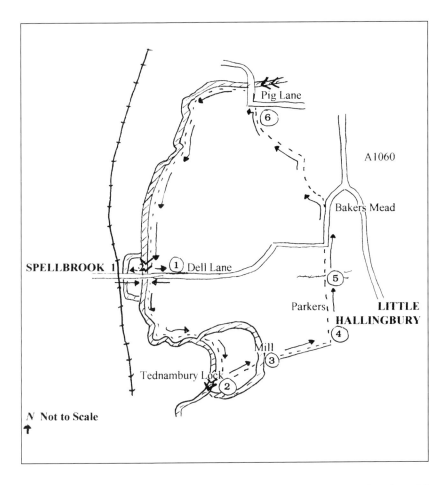

3. Cross the wooden and metal bridge over what looks like the old river course and descend into the private car park of Hallingbury Mill. This is now run as a business and conference centre and unfortunately is therefore not open to casual passers by. There is a concrete footpath sign just as you come down the steps. Cross the car park to walk uphill with the mill on your left-hand side. This interesting building dates back to 1874.

4. Walk up Mill Lane and just after number 3 turn left on a gravel track. It is marked with a footpath sign on which is painted '20'. The track takes you into 'Parkers'. As the brick wall on your right ends a grass track takes you ahead. There is no confirming arrow here, you have to

Passing through the lock at Tednambury

walk about another 100 yards and enter an unmown section before a yellow arrow on a post on your right confirms your route. In 100 yards you enter the corner of a field. Continue ahead with the hedge on your right and ignore the stile with yellow arrows that appears halfway down this hedge. When the trees run out the path goes straight ahead across the field to the bridge over the stream. You may see some locals continue down the field edge and at the end of the field turn left to make their way back to the bridge but this is not the true right of way.

5. Cross the bridge and stile and follow the yellow arrow up the hill to the next stile, another arrow and another wide well-defined uphill cross-field path. This takes you to a stile and the road. Continue walking in the same direction. The parish notice board confirms you are in Little Hallingbury. Just past Bakers Mead turn left down a gravel drive and after 10 feet, at a footpath sign, take the path on your right beside the fence. At the end of the field ignore left and right turns and carry on ahead into the woods. You soon come to a yellow arrow. Your path continues in the same direction passing many gates before it turns into a gravel track. At a crossing track continue ahead to Latchmead. You now cross half-left in front of the house to enter a large open field and walk downhill on a cross-field path with superb views.

6. As you come to two cottages the path continues straight ahead through the garden of the second one. Walk just to the right of the house to a gate in the corner. This leads onto the bridge over the stream. Cross the stile, field and another stile and turn left into Pig Lane. Take the footpath left before the canal. It is marked Stort Walk Way, Lee and Stort Navigations. Through the kissing gate walk with the canal on your right for about 1 mile back to Spellbrook Lock and your car.

PLACES OF INTEREST NEARBY
Hatfield Forest, at Hatfield Broad Oak, is a rare survival of a medieval royal hunting forest. There are also two ornamental lakes and the 18th-century Shell House, a cafe etc. Open all year, there is an admission charge for car parking. Telephone 01279 870678. Adventuress Cruises, The Maltings Island, Station Road, Sawbridgeworth run public cruises along the *River Stort*. Telephone 01279 600848 for details.

THAXTED AND THE INFANT RIVER CHELMER

❧❀❧

Enjoy the company of the tiny River Chelmer on this not-to-be-missed walk from Thaxted, the small medieval town that must be one of the jewels in the crown of Essex. Meadows, woods, an old forge and a restored windmill are just some of the delights along your route.

Folly Mill

The little River Chelmer flows just to the west of the ancient market town of Thaxted. In the Middle Ages the town enjoyed great prosperity from wool and cutlery. Today it is the beauty of its old buildings and its setting in the Essex countryside that draw thousands of visitors every year. The church must be one of the finest in the county and you have superb views of it from out in the open countryside and pass close by on your return to the town, so a visit is a must. You also pass the

26

windmill that is Thaxted's other great landmark. It was built in 1804 by John Webb, though there had been a windmill on the site since at least the 14th century. Field paths, streams and woods take you out to Bardfield End Green, Richmond's Green and Sibley's Green and all are remarkable in their own quiet way. Monk Street with its forge, inn and Folly Mill also has a lot to offer and the Glendale Forge, with its narrow gauge railway, may be another attraction you would like to visit on your walk (for details of this and the windmill, see Places of Interest below).

The Naughty but Nice Tea Shop at 10 Watling Street, Thaxted provides interesting meals at lunch times as well as the fare implied by its name (telephone 01371 831141). At the southern end of the town at the bottom of Thaxted hill is the Star. It has a warm, welcoming atmosphere and the landlord is very obliging. He welcomes walkers and provides excellent meals from omelettes through to fish dishes and specials. Telephone 01371 830368.

- **HOW TO GET THERE:** Thaxted lies at the junction of the B184 and B1051, about 6 miles north of Great Dunmow.
- **PARKING:** Make for the conspicuous spire of the church in Thaxted. Opposite, at the left-hand side of the Swan Hotel, is Margaret Street. Go down it to the car park on the left for free parking.
- **LENGTH OF THE WALK:** 5½ miles. Map: OS Landranger 167 Chelmsford, Harlow and surrounding area (GR 611312).

THE WALK

1. From the car park turn left along Margaret Street to Weaverhead Lane, turning right downhill. At the bottom turn left along Copthall Lane. Soon a path leads into Walnut Tree Meadow. Continue in your previous direction on a path with a hedge and stream on your left. At a gap in the trees turn left through them and cross a plank bridge. Soon waymarks appear and turn right along the banks of the stream. Carry straight on at a further arrow to follow a pebbly road.

2. Turn right at arrows, south-east, past a stile. Keep straight on at the hedge end, following the telegraph poles. Observe the view of Thaxted church away to the right. Join a hedge on your left leading to the road. Turn left for about 150 yards. Turn right at a house named 'The Yard'. Pass Greenhill Cottages, then two magnificent farm ponds at Hunts Farm and Freemans Farm. See the Victorian post box set into the wall on your right. Turn left along a road to Bardfield End Green.

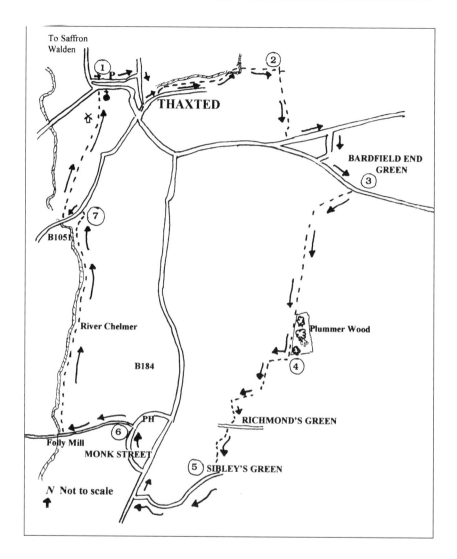

3. Turn right over the green past the cricket pavilion (Thaxted Cricket Club). Join a path on the right at a concrete public footpath sign, through a thicket to a field. Follow the arrow to the right and left at the field corner, following the path south. This path changes sides by the hedge twice on its way to Plummer Wood.

4. Past the wood turn right on a track, turning left with the track to Richmond's Green Farm. Turn right at the arrow. Turn left at the next

Thaxted and the route back to the church

arrow through farm buildings to a public footpath sign. Turn right to a road. Follow this road for 200 yards. Turn left at a footpath sign to walk along a good wide path to Sibley's Green.

5. Here you turn right uphill along what appears to be an old settlement, leading out to the B184. Cross with care and follow the sign to Monk Street. Again there are many interesting buildings, in particular the Glendale Forge with its miniature railway. You may wish to break your journey and visit the Farmhouse Inn with its excellent range of food and drink.

6. The walk continues by turning left to Folly Mill. Just before reaching the River Chelmer turn right over a stile (100 yards beyond on the road there are some very pretty buildings). After the stile there is a wired section close by the river and leading to a second and third stile. Soon the windmill and church at Thaxted come into view. Turn right round a field edge and left at a yellow arrow. Keep on the field edge to a bridge on the left.

7. Cross this bridge and turn left down the road. Just past the cottage turn right at a concrete public footpath sign. Climb the hill to the windmill. Finally, walk past the pretty almshouses and the church. To the left of the Swan Hotel a little road leads downhill past the toilets back to the car park.

PLACES OF INTEREST NEARBY

Glendale Forge at Monk Street displays hand-wrought blacksmith ironwork items and a private collection of half-size vehicles and fairground organs; 2 feet narrow gauge railway. Open all year Monday to Friday and Sunday morning. Telephone 01371 830466.

Thaxted Pottery, Crafts and Tea Room. Telephone 01371 830700 for opening details.

Thaxted Guildhall, Town Street is a 14th century timber-framed town hall and trading post, which regularly holds craft weekends. Open summer time only. Telephone 01371 831339.

John Webb's Windmill, a brick tower mill built 1804 with a small museum. Telephone 01371 830285 for opening details, usually 2 pm to 6 pm weekends and bank holidays 1st May to 30th September.

HIGH ONGAR AND THE RIVER RODING

៚ೕೕ៚

A lovely walk along the valley of the River Roding near High Ongar,
enjoying the peace and beauty of the riverbank and views across the
valley towards neighbouring Chipping Ongar.

High Ongar church

The River Roding rises at Molehill Green near Great Dunmow and
flows gently south towards the Thames, passing through its namesakes
the Rodings on the way. It passes under High Ongar Bridge on the road
from Chipping Ongar to Chelmsford. This walk is in a lovely area along
the Roding valley between Fyfield and Ongar where spotting birds,
butterflies and fish adds to the pleasure of the scenery. There are good
views towards Chipping Ongar from the ridge north of the A414, as
you walk towards Little Forest Hall and Tun Bridge, and the return
route is by the riverside along the Essex Way back to High Ongar. Since

the village was bypassed on the A414 the village street has assumed a quiet atmosphere and opportunities for parking near the church are fairly plentiful. The church has an interesting Norman doorway and a good brass in the floor of the nave. The lancet windows of the chancel show that the east end of the church was entirely rebuilt in the 13th century.

For such a small village High Ongar boasts good facilities. There is the village shop, Brenda's Mini Market, where a selection of convenience foods and drinks for a picnic can be bought. At the other end of the spectrum is a fine restaurant, The Mulberry Tree. Here it may be better to telephone in advance to ensure opening times: 01277 365832. The Red Lion pub, next door to the local school, prides itself on its hot meals and friendly atmosphere. Telephone 01277 362733.

- **HOW TO GET THERE:** Coming from the west or east along the A414, turn off as signposted to High Ongar and soon arrive at the church.
- **PARKING:** Park on the road or opposite the restaurant by the church.
- **LENGTH OF THE WALK:** 3¾ miles. Map: OS Landranger 167 Chelmsford, Harlow and surrounding area (GR 565038).

THE WALK

1. Walk eastward through the village. Just before the Forester's Arms turn left by a footpath direction post along a track between the pub and a house next door. Cross a stile at the boundary of the pub and continue over the field to the bypass. Over another stile, go down the steps, cross the road and go up the steps into the field ahead. Cross the field towards the left edge of the wood ahead. Follow a grassy path with the wood on your right.

2. At the second waymark arrow, turn right on to a concrete path. Pass West Park Lodge and 150 yards on turn left past cottages leading to Little Forest Hall. Walk through the farm buildings and through an avenue of fir trees. Cross a field and pass a wood on your left. Cross the next field down to the right edge of the hedge and pass through the hedge corner. Follow the field edge with a hedge on your right. Turn left, crossing the field, then right and left over a ditch and walk back to Tun Bridge ahead.

3. Cross the bridge and follow the Essex Way left along the bank of the River Roding. Cross over a plank bridge, then a single plank and a three

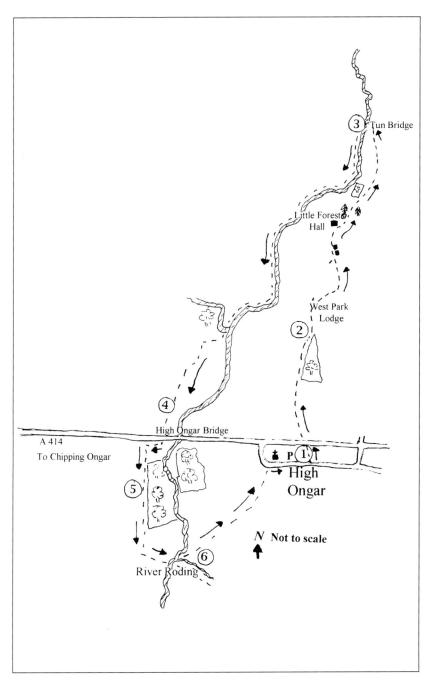

③ Tun Bridge

Little Forest
Hall

West Park
Lodge

②

④

High Ongar Bridge

A 414
To Chipping Ongar

P ①

➤ High
Ongar

⑤

N **Not to scale**

⑥

River Roding

On the bank of the River Roding

plank crossing. More plank bridges follow as you make your way south by river. About a mile from Tun Bridge cross a stile by a plank bridge (another!) and continue close to the river over another stile to a meadow. Most Ordnance Survey maps show this section of the Essex Way 50 yards to the north across an arable field. The diversion closer to the river took place some years ago so follow the signs till the map catches up.

4. At the end of the meadow branch half-right to a gate by the main road (the A414). Climb over the stile and cross the side road. Bear left to walk under the High Ongar Bridge. Turn right and follow the path west to descend steps on your left, continuing by the side of the field to the corner.

5. Turn left along the track, passing a wood on your left. When you come to a stile on your right turn left on a path and walk to the bridge 100 yards on to cross the River Roding once again.

6. Take the path forking to the left and walk uphill towards the school, emerging on the road near the road junction in High Ongar. You are now near the church and will quickly regain your car.

PLACES OF INTEREST NEARBY
In nearby *Chipping Ongar* is a little room where the 19th-century missionary-explorer David Livingstone lived, serving his probation before he set out on his lifework in Africa. From long before his time is a mound today crowned by trees where once stood the wooden keep of a Norman castle. Yet certainly it dates from before the Conqueror's time for there is a medley of Roman tiles in its walls, put there by the Saxons. The mound is 230 feet across encircled by a moat 50 feet wide, with the water still in it. The site of a rampart 80 feet wide has been traced embracing the whole of Ongar, a remarkable example of a town enclosure of feudal days.
Greensted Church at Greensted, west of Chipping Ongar, is the oldest wooden church in the world, dating from the 11th century. It is open all year dawn to dusk, admission is free. Telephone 01277 364694 for more information.

WRITTLE AND THE RIVERS WID AND CAN
❧❀❧

An enjoyable walk which follows the River Wid from the historic settlement of Writtle to its confluence with the River Can and Chelmsford's Admiral's Park, in the footsteps of King John and of the pioneers of modern radio broadcasting.

The duck pond at Writtle

To the east of Chelmsford the River Wid flows into the Can, before they both become part of the Chelmer. Writtle is the ideal place to begin this walk of two rivers. It is an ancient settlement which has been in existence since Roman times and was given the right to hold a market in 1199. Today it has the appearance of much ordered grandeur, many of its older buildings surrounding the ancient green. Your walk today starts near Wear Pond. Water flows into the pond from pipes connected to a large canal system in the garden of Motts. In 1866 the law required a supply of water for traction engines to be provided every 800 yards in a built up area so this is one of 14 ponds known to have been in the area at that time. You will walk as far into Chelmsford as Admiral's Park before crossing the river and returning along its northern bank to join Lawford Lane. This now pleasant bridleway was part of the main route between London and East Anglia in the times when travellers made a detour to avoid crossing the marshy River Can at Chelmsford. The lane was once known as Lollefordstrat. It may well have been used by King John who built his hunting lodge in Writtle in 1211. On your return route into Writtle you pass the site of the Marconi Hut that transmitted Britain's first regular public broadcast. On 14th February 1922 it was licensed for one half hour programme a week and broadcast under the call sign 2MT Two Emma Toc. There is a heritage plaque outside Melba Court in Lawford Lane giving much more information for you to read when you make your visit.

There is a wide choice of eating places in Writtle. The fish and chip shop may tempt you away from the excellent pubs. The Inn on the Green is an old, large establishment and is excellent for a full meal (telephone 01245 420266) or there is the smaller but pleasant Wheatsheaf (telephone 01245 420695). Or maybe the Indian restaurant is more your choice. For those visiting on a Tuesday, make sure you visit the excellent fresh fish van. His crabs are well worth taking home for tea. Although phone numbers have been given, perhaps you are best served by walking round the green and making your own choice on the day. If you have children with you remember the ducks on the pond would like feeding if you have any suitable bread!

- **HOW TO GET THERE:** Writtle lies just to the west of Chelmsford, our county town. Make your way onto the A414 and about 1½ miles past Widford church turn right to enter the village from the south. For those coming from West Essex turn left from the A414 at the Margaretting Road roundabout. At the school turn right, then left when you reach the T junction by the Cock and Bell pub.
- **PARKING:** The car park is clearly signed to the left of the green. There is no charge for using the public car park, which has good toilets just by the exit.
- **LENGTH OF THE WALK:** 2¾ miles. Map: OS Landranger 167 Chelmsford, Harlow and surrounding area (GR 677062).

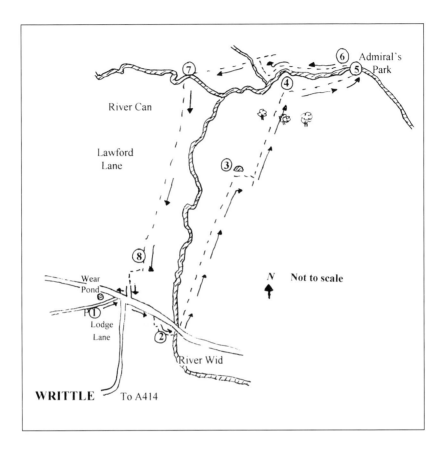

THE WALK

1. Walk out of the car park towards Wear Pond. Turn right and cross Lodge Road. Walk in front of the Cock and Bell and the fish and chip shop. When you come to the Co-op turn right and then left to exit from the side rear of their car park. This takes you down to the banks of the River Wid. Turn left and walk along the bank on the new Chelmsford Council footpath.

2. At the road turn right and cross Writtle Bridge, built in 1891 by Westwood Baillie and Co Ltd, Engineers of London. Cross the road with care and take the footpath opposite. It has a concrete footpath sign. Your route is up a gravel drive, walking with hedges on either side. Ignore a right-hand turn and continue ahead to a metal gate. Go over the stile beside the locked gate to enter a large field. Walk with the

The pillar bridge over the River Can by Admiral's Park

hedge on your right. At wooden railings go over a second stile.

3. At the field corner turn right at a gap in the hedge, climbing over the metal bar stile. Walk to the right of the pond. As a footpath joins from the right, turn left and take the crossfield path towards willow trees. Walk under cables by a pole marked '3', then descend into a spinney across which you join the banks of the River Can.

4. Turn right and walk past Beach Mills G.S. and then cross the sub-river on a bridge of brick and grass. Continue with the river on your left. You can take the tarred path from Beach Mills if it is wet underfoot.

5. Turn left over a brick and pillar bridge into Admiral's Park and left again to walk back along the other side of the River Can. Admiral's Park is a good place for an apple stop; there are children's climbing toys and toilets.

6. The public footpath leaves the river at the post and follows along the back gardens of houses and through the housing estate. You can take this if you wish. However, on a sunny day you can do as the locals do and follow the river bank to Beach Mills and then the narrow path, taking the right fork that takes you past the end of some gardens to rejoin the public footpath at a brown and white marker post.

7. Turn left to cross the stream on a metal bridge. Walk away from the stream with the hedge on your right. Ignore paths right into the playing fields. Cross a stile at a direction post and continue straight on, crossing over a track. Cross the footbridge over the River Can to enter Lawford Lane. Ignore several paths turning off on your right and after ½ mile come to a gate leading out onto the road. Just to your left is Melba Court, once the site of Marconi's Hut. You will find the plaque nearly hidden behind the road sign.

8. Now make your way round the bend along the housed end of Lawford Lane to St John's Green. The ancient market and fairs were held near here. Turn left, and a yellow arrow confirms your route back to the Cock and Bell, the green and your car.

PLACES OF INTEREST NEARBY

The remains of *King John's hunting lodge* and moat are on the edge of the village in the grounds of Writtle College. Telephone 01245 420705 for permission to visit. *Hylands Park* is 500 acres of parkland including lawns and formal gardens, home of the Chelmsford Spectacular and 'V' Festivals in the summer. The recently restored Hylands House is open to the public and has a programme of events. Telephone 01245 606396. *Moulsham Mill*, Parkway, Chelmsford is an 18th-century water mill housing craft workshops and small businesses. Admission free. Telephone 01245 608200. *Chelmsford Cathedral* has been a place of worship for 1,200 years, and the 15th-century building now on the site is home of the May music festival. Telephone 01245 420100. *Chelmsford & Essex and Essex Regiment Museums*, Oaklands Park, Moulsham Street, Chelmsford have displays of both local and natural history, plus ceramics, costumes, coins and glass. Telephone 01245 353066.

WALK 8

COALHOUSE FORT AND THE RIVER THAMES

Ships large and small are part of the scenery as you walk the banks of the River Thames from the Elizabethan Coalhouse Fort at East Tilbury. History and the ever-fascinating Thames combine to make this an intriguing stroll.

Looking across the River Thames to Kent

East Tilbury has been a thriving settlement since its establishment in the 1st century AD as a crossing place of the Thames. The foundations of a group of ancient huts used to be visible on the foreshore. St Cedd built a church here in AD 653. At one time locals claimed an old coffin slab was his although he is known to have died in Yorkshire. The little church that stands today is mostly late 12th and 13th-century. It was fired on by Dutch ships in 1667 and repaired by bored soldiers from nearby Coalhouse Fort garrison during the First World War. Coalhouse

41

Fort itself was built by Queen Elizabeth I as part of a complex system of coastal defences to protect London from invasion. In the years I have been visiting the Fort it has been extensively restored, so do visit if you can. The walk starts by looping round the fort then heading north along the banks of the rather wide River Thames. You are about 22 miles from the river mouth and most certainly will be entertained as you make your way along the banks of the Thames by a parade of ships, from containers to large cruise liners. On reaching Linford you have a road walk passing the Bata shoe factory and a surprisingly green area of playing fields. You now head for Buckland Farm and another stream that guides you along Footpath 200 all the way back to Coalhouse Fort.

The Ship, a free house in Princess Margaret Road just up from the fort, is your nearest pub. It carries a wide range of beers and food choices include sandwiches, omelettes, steak and kidney pie, gammon and chicken kiev. Telephone 01375 843041. On a sunny day you may prefer to bring a picnic and have it in the outer grounds of the fort or you may be lucky enough to visit on an open day and take refreshment in the fort's cafe.

- **HOW TO GET THERE:** Make your way to the A13 between Orsett, the A128 junction, and Stanford le Hope, the B1007 junction. Now look for the signs to the old A13 currently known as the A1013. Just over a mile from its easterly or westerly joining point you will see a road signed going south to Linford, East Tilbury with a brown sign to Coalhouse Fort. Follow the road right through till you come to Coalhouse Fort.
- **PARKING:** Park in the large car park in front of Coalhouse Fort (free).
- **LENGTH OF THE WALK:** 6½ miles. Map: OS Landranger 177 East London area or 178 The Thames Estuary (GR 689768).

THE WALK

1. From the car park turn right and walk in front of the toilets and the fort, keeping them on your left. You have good views of the River Thames and its traffic and there are plenty of seats if you just want to sit and watch for a while. Just as the car park comes into view on your left, turn right on a grass track to steps.

2. Turn left to visit St Catherine's church and return to this point, or just turn right onto a concrete path to the right of the sea defences. Follow this concrete defence path about 2 miles heading north up the

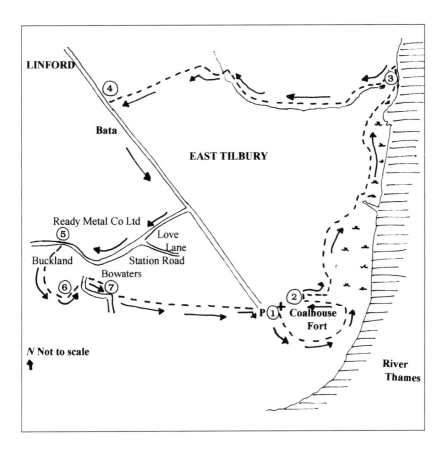

banks of the Thames. You will notice the interesting concrete duck ramps up the sea defence wall, also the pampas grasses that give such interest to the salt marshes you pass. Where a track crosses the sea defences, go right and left onto the track and right again over the track to descend back onto the concrete path. It is a very steep descent for a couple of steps.

3. As the concrete wall and path end turn left beside a high wire fence. Walk to the right of a pond and, as it appears, to the right of a stream. Follow between the stream and the wire fence on a grassed track for ½ mile till you come to an earth bridge over the stream. A sign on the gates to your right tells you Thurrock Footpath 147 has been diverted from its original route that is now part of the landfill and gravel site. Turn left over the bridge and follow the gravel hedged track. It

43

Coalhouse Fort

becomes tarred then sanded as you walk to the right of a housing estate. You go through a kissing gate just to the right of a wooden gate as you reach the footpath sign and the road.

4. Turn left and walk down the road. There is a handy Londis shop if, like me, you fancy a cold drink at this point. Walking on you pass the Bata Shoe company and the traffic calming measure you drove through to get to the start of the walk. Turn right into Love Lane. The narrow road has one-way traffic so take care. This becomes Station Road as a road joins from your left and two-way traffic resumes. As a concrete track goes straight on, the road turns right. Go with it till just at the start of a bend nearly opposite Ready Metal Co Ltd you will find a footpath sign on the left.

5. Cross the gate into a meadow and walk with the hedge on your left. The map shows the path as going behind the pond but this is impassable so we must do as the locals do. Keep between the hedge on the left and the one on the right that soon appears. When you come to the stile in the corner near a blue paint and wire gate, beware of the barbed wire on the stile as you cross. Follow a faint line of an old track, you have a dried up stream on your right. The track turns south, then south-east and becomes too overgrown to walk. Make your way as those before have done onto the field edge and continue up this till you reach a gravel track.

6. Turn left up the track. In 40 yards a concrete road joins from your right. Just before the green gates up the hill in front of you is a green and white footpath post, indicating the path goes right into some rather dense undergrowth. If the path has not been cleared on the day you walk it I suggest you retrace your steps. Follow the concrete road that joined from your right until it comes to a sharp right bend. This is where the footpath you abandoned comes out. On your left is a track up to some farm buildings and ahead a cable pole marked IF81 with a 290 just above it.

7. Keep to this path ahead. It follows under the cables and to the left bank of the stream. The path has recently been cut by the council, I am told. You come to a large field. Head across this and climb up the slope at its northern end. Turn left. You are now on a grass track that passes a sea defence wall then turns slightly right downhill, then left as it brings you to the road. The footpath sign telling you that you have walked Footpath 200 confirms your way. Turn right to your car which you should have already spotted in the car park.

PLACES OF INTEREST NEARBY
Coalhouse Fort has historical displays and occasional demonstrations. There is a cafe at the fort. For opening days and special events details telephone 01375 844203. *Tilbury Fort* is a star-shaped, 17th-century gem of military engineering. It was near this spot Queen Elizabeth made the famous Armada Address. Telephone 01375 858489 for opening times. At *Thurrock Museum*, Thameside Complex, Orsett Road, Grays, local history and archaeology are on display. Telephone 01375 382555 for details of when it's open, they do organise guided tours by special arrangement. *Walton Hall Farm and Museum*, Walton Hall Road, Linford, signed from the route you used coming to East Tilbury, has farm animals and farm and other bygones. Telephone 01375 671874.

TWO TREE ISLAND

An island of two halves at the mouth of the River Thames, Two Tree Island offers a country park and a bird watcher's paradise. Wonderful views accompany this walk which is never far from the water, overlooked by a ruined castle.

Two Tree Island seen from Leigh on Sea

Two Tree Island nestles below ruined Hadleigh Castle. The Country Park extends over the bridge to the Castle Point end of the island, while the eastern end is an Essex Wildlife Trust Nature Reserve. From the nature reserve there are fine views over Leigh Marsh to the Leigh cockle sheds and Southend Pier, while to the south you look across Canvey Point, Leigh Middle and the River Thames to the Isle of Grain. Leaving the nature reserve to pass the busy boating centre and car park on your way into the Country Park, as you walk along the southern banks of the island views over Hadleigh Bay and Benfleet Creek enable you to get a close up of Canvey Island. The path around the Lagoon is fun but was unfortunately closed when we walked out this circuit. You should find time, however, to stop in the hide to see some of the birds that visit the area.

I would recommend a visit to Old Leigh for your refreshments. You can either walk from the car park or take your car back past Leigh Station, then right and right again to park on the bridge or, on a very quiet day, in Old Leigh itself. Visitors will find a wide variety of food on offer. Amongst the array of pubs you may like the small old fashioned unspoilt Crooked Billet. Here you may expect to find a wide range of sandwiches, baguettes, jacket potatoes, fish meals plus a blackboard menu. The usual range of hand pump bitters, ciders etc are available. It does tend to get very busy at weekends in the summer (telephone 01702 714854). Another favourite of mine is The Smack Inn. It has a veranda facing the estuary where you can sit to enjoy some of their excellent meals. If you are looking for a more substantial meal you may prefer to go here. There is the usual range of drinks on offer that satisfy the most demanding of regular customers! Telephone 01702 476765 for more information or to book. For those looking for tea rooms or an ice cream just wander along the High Street till you come to one you fancy. If you like shellfish go no further than Osborne Brothers at Billet Wharf where you can get anything from local crabs to cockles, mussels, jellied eels, roll mops etc. If you want to phone ahead an order for a take away telephone 01702 477233.

- **HOW TO GET THERE:** Two Tree Island is behind Leigh on Sea station. Take the A13 (East) to London Road, turn south into Thames Drive. Go straight across the traffic lights in Marine Parade, down Belton Way to Leigh station. Turn right to pass the station on your right and continue on the back road for about ¾ mile, crossing over Leigh Creek bridge.
- **PARKING:** Park in the first car park on your left after the bridge. It is opposite the entrance marked 'Hadleigh Castle Country Park Two Tree Island'.
- **LENGTH OF THE WALK:** 2¾ miles. Map: OS Landranger 178 The Thames Estuary (GR 825853).

THE WALK

1. Leave the car park heading south to go over paving stones to join a green path. After 75 yards turn left to enter Two Tree Island Nature Reserve. You go through a kissing gate and walk past the Wardens Hut.

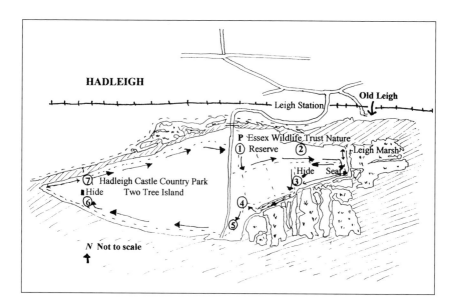

Take the path ahead towards Southend on Sea. The path crosses a junction of paths, you continue ahead passing Roy's Spinney where there is a drinking fountain.

2. A path joins from the left. Ignore this for the present but note the post with the yellow arrow for your use when you return here shortly. Your path goes down a slight dip and bears round to the right, then you come to the end of the Island. The path to your left is closed but to your right you will see a concrete bunker with a seat beside it. Head for this and a rest while you watch the birds visiting Leigh Marsh ahead of you. The path on the south of the island is closed for some 300 yards so retrace your steps to the yellow arrow post you noted just now. For keen bird watchers there is a hide on your left just before this you may care to visit. Turn left up this track, part of a wildlife walk, and after 100 yards you come to the sea wall.

3. Turn right along the sea wall. The closed footpath joins from your left at the direction post. Continue along this south bank of the island with a dyke on your right and the marshes on your left. The views here are over the Thames to Kent.

4. Ignore the next direction post at the end of this sea wall section to the wildlife walk, which turns right near the edge of the reserve. You keep left and cross a stile. Turn left again and head out onto the road.

5. Walk south for 75 yards and cross to the left of the car park. You are heading for the kissing gate in the far corner and the continuation of the sea wall path. Your path passes a number of picnic tables and seats as you walk towards the lagoon.

6. Just before the lagoon turn right and you will find the bird hide. Time for another stop. You may have brought your binoculars and be able to get a better look at the wading birds who like to visit the lagoon. After your visit continue on the path north till you come to the stile and muddy crossing to the mainland.

7. At this point do not cross to the mainland, turn right and take the grass track that runs nearest to the south side of Leigh Creek. You will have good views over to Hadleigh Castle and walk past another seat. Keep on this path as it heads back along the northern edge of the island. When you can see the back of the Hadleigh Country Park information board head for this and the kissing gate that brings you back to the road. Cross to your waiting car.

PLACES OF INTEREST NEARBY

Leigh Heritage Centre at 13a High Street, Old Leigh, is a former blacksmith's. Admission free. For opening times call 01702 470834.
Hadleigh Castle Country Park's fields and woodlands overlook the Thames Estuary. Access via Chapel Lane. Parking fees charged on Sundays and Bank Holidays. Entrance free. Telephone 01702 551072. Footpaths from here lead to the ruins of the castle built for Edward III. Admission free.

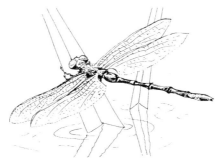

SOUTH WOODHAM FERRERS – RIVER AND CREEKS

Smugglers used the creeks and inlets of the River Crouch to hide their contraband in days past, but today the river provides the setting for an easy and relaxing walk by the water, just below South Woodham Ferrers.

Looking upstream along the River Crouch

The River Crouch rises to the south of Billericay and then flows to the sea along the southern edge of the Dengie Peninsula. How lucky the residents of the new town of South Woodham Ferrers are to have such a beautiful river walk as this right on their doorstep. Walking east on the banks of the Crouch, on the far bank is the Brandy Hole Sailing Club (I was a member in the late 1950s!). It is said to have been the place smugglers temporarily ditched their brandy casks only to come back and recover them when the coast was clear. You will pass Brandy Hole

Reach before turning into Clementsgreen Creek. As in so many estuaries with their numerous inlets, you have to walk round Hawbush Creek to rejoin Clementsgreen Creek before you leave the sea wall. Your path just one field south of the new town is surprisingly delightful. In the spring lambs and their mothers give the walker much to enjoy. You then pass Marsh Farm Country Park, where over the fence you are often able to glimpse sheep, goats and other farm animals.

When you are ready to eat you may choose the cafe at Marsh Farm, especially if you are to make a visit as part of your day out. My favourite pub is the Whalebone in Old Wickford Road off the B1012. They do a wide range of Indian curries and sweet and sour dishes and children's meals. The selection of beers includes Greene King and Kronenbourg 1664, the normal range of ciders etc is also available. Telephone 01245 320231.

- **HOW TO GET THERE:** From the A130 at Rettendon Turnpike about 5 miles south-east of Chelmsford, take the B1012 east for about 1½ miles till you come to Shaw Farm roundabout. Marsh Farm Country Park is well signed with brown boards through the new town of South Woodham Ferrers. Follow these signs till you come to the farm in Marsh Farm Road, then take the narrow road ahead down to the riverside.
- **PARKING:** In the riverside car park (free).
- **LENGTH OF THE WALK:** 3¾ miles. Map: OS Landranger 168 Colchester and the Blackwater (GR 809957).

THE WALK

1. Turn left from the car park, cross over the road to a concrete direction post and go through the kissing gate. Walk in front of the sailing club on the sea wall. This path passes a seat as you go towards a second kissing gate. You will see Marsh Farm on your left, and Bushey Hill with its communications station is also high on the hill behind it. As you pass Brandy Hole on the far river bank you go through a kissing gate marked South Woodham Ring. Ignore the path left and continue east along the sea wall. You will soon be able to spot the water tower at Cold Norton and the white spire of Stow Maries church.

2. As the path turns left you will see the pontoon at the entrance to Clementsgreen Creek. To the north-east behind the railway nestles

51

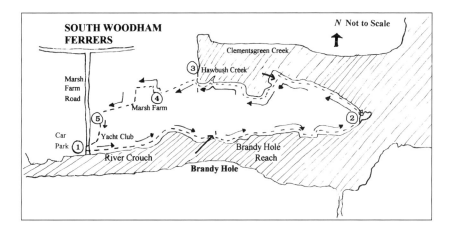

Skinners Wick, no relation I am sorry to say. Soon the roofs of South Woodham Ferrers come into view in the distance. This new town was planned in the 1970s and built on what was once marshy land in the parish of its much older namesake, the village of Woodham Ferrers. When a figure 8 appears in the creek you turn left and walk the wall round Hawbush Creek. At the steps turn right and go through the kissing gate. The yellow arrow confirms your way is straight on. As you reach the point, you can either walk the river bank or follow the local short cut to rejoin the path some 50 yards further on. Follow the short section of the sea wall to a gate with a kissing gate to its right. A yellow arrow again confirms your way.

3. As the sea wall continues ahead you turn left down a rutted green lane. There is a fence on your left and a dyke on the right and you are one field back from the outskirts of the town. You pass a white bungalow on your right. It is said to have stood there long before the new town was thought of. The lane becomes a concrete track as you continue straight ahead. At the slurry pit it bends slightly rightish.

4. You soon enter the country park and take the stile on your right. Walk between the fences with a dyke on your left. You then follow the field edge right and walk towards the houses. Near the end of the field turn left with a hedge on your right. Turn left towards the gate marked 'No entry to Farm Buildings'. Turn right and walk the footpath passing the farm trail and children's play and picnic area on your left. This brings you to the rear of the gift shop and tea rooms. Turn left to the entrance to Marsh Farm.

Looking across the river to Hullbridge

Those of you wishing to make a visit can choose to do so now and finish the walk back to the car later. (see Places of Interest below).

5. Make your way to the far left-hand side of Marsh Farm car park and just before the car exit you will see a little gap in the hedge on your left. Go through this and you will see an arrow. Follow this route across the concrete track to another yellow arrow on a post. You walk south between two wired fences till you come to the field corner where the kissing gate on your left brings you out just before the South Woodham Ferrers Ski Club and Yacht Club. Go over the concrete road and ahead uphill passing a direction post at the road. Cross the road and walk back up to the car park and your car.

PLACES OF INTEREST NEARBY
Marsh Farm Country Park is a modern working farm with piggery and sheep, and a pets corner with rabbits, goats, chickens etc plus a farm trail. Special events are laid on throughout the year. For more information telephone 01245 321552.

BURNHAM ON CROUCH AND THE SALTINGS

❧❀❧

From the bustling yachtman's paradise of Burham on Crouch to the lonely saltings teeming with birdlife, this fascinating walk has something for everyone. Don't forget your binoculars to make the most of the opportunities for birdspotting.

Burnham marina

Burnham is the leading boating centre in Essex and has been so for many years. In addition a yacht harbour was created about ten years ago for access to the sea at all stages of the tide. Those of you with sharp eyes will spot the lifeboat station in the harbour. It was created here in 1997 and is remarkable in that it goes up and down with the tide so the boat can be launched promptly whenever an emergency arises. At the same time as the harbour was constructed a country park was built, partly from the soil dug out of the marina. The church is a mile back from the river behind a green and by a farm. At the corners of the porch are two monstrous grotesques and on a buttress is a medieval scratch dial. On the wall of the chapel is a tablet set up in memory of his family by Dr Alexander Scott who was vicar of Southminster a few miles away. He is remembered as the chaplain of the *Victory* and it was into his ears the dying Nelson murmured, 'Thank God, I have done my duty'. This walk takes you from the marina, right along the sea front through Burnham and out through its east end. This may be a flat area but it's never dull. Here you will discover the difference between mere reclaimed marsh and true saltings. The land is richly productive and some of the loneliest in southern England. As you walk along the sea wall you will no doubt find on your right much to catch your interest. Sailing races pass this way, as do the many sea birds who live on and visit the river Crouch. It is at this point we turn inland and return via the very interesting High Street to the hustle and bustle of this yachtsman's paradise.

In the town centre are several pubs and restaurants for your nourishment after the walk. The Ship Inn at 52 High Street can be particularly recommended. It is a pleasant open pub with excellent snacks and a full blackboard of meals. It also carries a wide range of beers and ciders. Telephone 01621 785057.

- **HOW TO GET THERE:** From Latchingdon and Althorne the B1010 leads onto the B1021 and Burnham on Crouch. Turn right past the railway station. Soon turn right along Foundry Lane and this leads into the park over several sleeping policemen. Just as you arrive at the marina turn left into the large car park.

  For those of you who wish to travel by train the station in Burnham is only about five minutes' walk from the marina so just follow the road right from the station down to Foundry Lane and into the park.
- **PARKING:** Park at the Yacht Harbour car park (free).
- **LENGTH OF THE WALK:** 5¼ miles. Map: OS Landranger 168 Colchester and the Blackwater (GR 945958).

THE WALK

1. From the car park descend steep steps down to the harbour. Turn left to walk round to the sea wall and left along the path towards Burnham. Pass the war memorial and in succession the Star, the White Hart and the Anchor, all offering access from the riverside as well as to the High Street. Continue along the Quay. As you come to the eastern

55

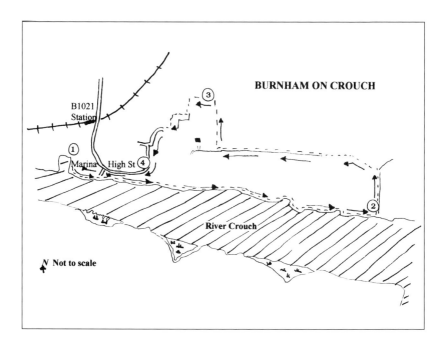

end of the town pass the famous Royal Burnham and Royal Corinthian Yacht Clubs. Now follow the River Crouch and ½ mile later walk round a cut to a wooden building. This is a hide for avid birdwatchers. On the far bank is Wallasea Island and behind this is an area for military testing and, as the map says, the Danger Area of Foulness Island.

2. Beyond the hide cross a stile. Soon after, turn left away from the sea wall and follow the track. When the track turns right bear left along the crop divide. After about ½ mile from the sea wall a large notice points left. Follow this, turning right with a public footpath sign.

3. Soon turn left again and follow the path past Burnham Wick to reach Wick Road. Turn right along this road and continue into Silver Road to the High Street. The mainly Georgian buildings give a feeling of years gone by, but because of its nearby quay and yacht club there are many chandlers shops and links with the water. The whole is dominated by the Victorian clock tower. It is here that you may wish to eat or drink according to the time.

4. The walk continues along the High Street, turning right as it goes.

The waterfront at Burnham on Crouch

Near a garage turn left into Remembrance Avenue. When this ends keep to the right of playing fields into the country park and make your way back to the marina and your car.

PLACES OF INTEREST NEARBY

Burnham on Crouch & District Museum, on the Quay, houses agricultural and maritime exhibits plus a collection of archaeological and social items. Open March to end November, Saturday, Sunday and bank holidays, and each day of Burnham Week (last week of August). Telephone 01621 782562. In Southminster Road is the *Mangapps Farm Railway Museum*. Youngsters of all ages will enjoy this extensive collection of railway relics, be their interest steam or diesel, carriages or wagons. Train rides are also available. Open most weekends from March to November. Sometimes 'Thomas and the Fat Controller' visit. Telephone 01621 784898.

BRADWELL ON SEA AND ST PETER'S CHAPEL

An exhilarating walk along the North Sea coast at Bradwell on Sea, with the added interest of an ancient chapel built on the site of a Roman fort.

St Peter's Chapel

The River Blackwater flows into the sea at Bradwell but this walk is a coastal one – with the added advantage around here that it can be taken in winter without the fear of getting stuck in the mud! The Romans were here and your route begins along part of the old Roman road. Then follows an interesting walk along the narrow winding road leading to Sandbeach Farm and on to the inner sea wall behind Dengie Flat. Having joined St Peter's Way the remaining route is along the edge of the North Sea to the old Roman fort on which the chapel stands. St Peter's Chapel has been a destination for pilgrims since it was built in

AD 654, when this spot was populated and busy around the old fort of Othona, one of the 'forts of the Saxon shore' with which the Romans protected the coast against sea raiders. Bishop (later Saint) Cedd led a mission here, helping to reintroduce Christianity to southern England. The little chapel has in its time been a Tudor lighthouse and a barn before it was reconsecrated in the 1920s.

There are two pubs in the village. We have eaten in both and had good food and drink in pleasant surroundings. The nearest is the Cricketers that you pass on the walk. This is slightly the smaller pub but it has a fine garden where you may wish to regain your strength on a warm sunny day! Telephone 01621 776013. The King's Head is in the village near the church. It has a couple of bars plus a large conservatory where you can eat in comfort. Telephone 01621 776224.

- **HOW TO GET THERE:** On the Dengie Peninsula, follow the brown signs to 'Bradwell Visitor Centre' as far as Latchingdon on the B1010. At the roundabout at the far end of the village take the road through Mayland and Steeple till after 10 miles you get to a garage. Turn right, signed to Bradwell Village, drive into the village centre then follow the brown signs 'St Peter's Chapel' through East End and down the Roman Road to Eastlands Farm.
- **PARKING:** There is a large public car park for the chapel just to the left of the farm.
- **LENGTH OF THE WALK:** 5½ miles. Map: OS Landranger 168 Colchester and the Blackwater (GR 023079).

THE WALK

1. Leave the car park, walking south-west back up the road you drove in on to get to the car park. You have good views over the Blackwater to West Mersea. After the entrance to Easthall Farm, Bradwell Power Station comes into view. This was one of the first commercial nuclear generating stations in Britain, built in the 1950s. As you pass Eastlands Cottage you start to get sightings of hangars on the old airfield. Next comes Eastland Caravan Park and its long-closed shop. Pass the Cricketers and the post box.

2. When you get opposite Dormer Cottage turn left into Hockley Lane. Walk along this lane under the power lines. At the farm make sure you do not miss the dog on the weather vane. The country lane turns from tar to concrete and a footpath sign confirms you can ignore the sign

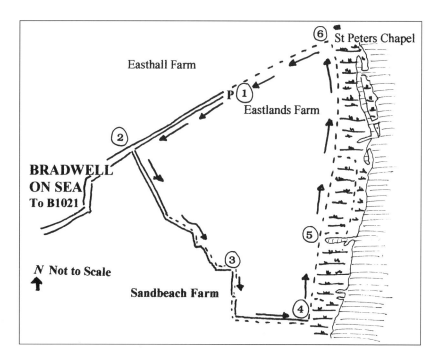

'Private Road No Unauthorised Vehicles Beyond This Point'. On pole 26 a yellow arrow confirms the way. At BT pole 31 pass between barns.

3. As the road turns right a yellow arrow confirms the route and you are heading for Sandbeach Farm. The outhouses are clearly visible. At the barns turn left, then right and head for the metal gate ahead. You pass the pretty white weatherboarded farm on your right, then pass by some large tanks. At the corner turn left. You will see to your right the footpath with the St Peter's Way sign. Two metal gates give access to a narrow tarred road with a ditch on the left and a wide grass verge on the right. You are making your way towards the masts.

4. As the road begins to climb, turn left and walk with the sparse trees on your left and open farmland on the right. The sea wall lies straight on. Here you have an option. If the weather is cold you may prefer to stay at the lower level on the track. If it is a fine day climb the bank to the post and continue ahead on the sea wall. The true St Peter's Way turns right, then left and left along the first creek to St Peter's Flat, and then returns inland just before Gunners Creek.

The path to the chapel

5. Continue along the sea wall or track to St Peter's Chapel. Just a few yards from the chapel to the right and hidden by trees is the rather isolated Linnett's Cottage. It was the home of Walter Linnett, a wildfowler and fisherman. He lived in this solitary cottage till his death in 1958. If you wish to pass the cottage bear right through the trees then across the field to the chapel. If you do make the detour, tread quietly as it is now the Bradwell Bird Observatory and most weekends is visited by a group of eager twitchers.

6. Your car is up the pebble track that leaves the chapel heading south-west.

PLACES OF INTEREST NEARBY
Bradwell Power Station has a hi-tech visitor centre, where you can decide between a visit to the power station and a nature walk. Admission free. Telephone 01621 873395. *St Lawrence's church* is situated on a hill overlooking the River Blackwater, signed from the B1010. It holds exhibitions in summer months. Telephone 01621 779319.

MAYLANDSEA AND THE
RIVER BLACKWATER
❧❀❧

Walk along the northern shore of the Dengie peninsula, where the River Blackwater flows to the sea, and enjoy the salt marshes and creeks, the boats and the birds.

The view to Mundon Creek from the marina

The Essex beer guide describes Maylandsea as a sprawling riverside development. This is true but it has much more to offer. Some householders enjoy the pleasure of living on Nipsells Chase not far from the waterside in houses and bungalows joined to the rest of the village by an unmade road. The gardens of the properties are rural to the extent foxes and many birds visit on a regular basis. I know someone who feeds the tame local birds currants by hand. Yachtsmen are attracted by Maylandsea's marina, boat chandlery and the more recently opened Hopper's Bar. Mayland is situated on the north side of the Dengie peninsula and lies in the Mundon Creek. Our route takes us down to the Creek, to walk north-east along the sea wall and along Lawling Creek. We turn south, just before the creeks join the River Blackwater, to walk along Mayland Creek to join the St Peter's Way for the last ¾ mile back to the car. As well as seeing all the boating, birds, and excellent salt marshes you have views across to Osea Island sitting proudly in the Blackwater and on a clear day, Stansgate Abbey the home of the Benn family.

My personal choice for pub food would be the welcoming Hopper's Bar. For some while they have extended their hospitality to walkers and are now on the visiting list of many groups in Essex. You can find them just to the right of the Marine Office down by the marina. Telephone 01621 741073. The General Lee in Imperial Avenue has the merit of being near your car. Telephone 01621 740791. Mayland Mill on the main road in Mayland offers more of a restaurant service with three course meals including a roast on Sundays and its famous sea food platters. Telephone 01621 740998 to book. There is also a Chinese restaurant by the garage in Mayland that trades by the name of The Rickshaw, telephone 01621 740278 for opening times and to book.

- **HOW TO GET THERE:** On the Dengie peninsula, from Latchingdon on the B1010 take the Steeple Road – the first exit at the roundabout at the east end of the village. After about 2 miles take the left turn just before the petrol station marked Maylandsea Marina. This road called Park Drive brings you to Imperial Avenue.
- **PARKING:** Park on the road near the shops, making sure you do not block anyone's drive.
- **LENGTH OF THE WALK:** 4 miles. Map: OS Landranger 168 Colchester and the Blackwater (GR 905022).

THE WALK

1. From the shops walk west, turning right down Marine Parade towards the water. When you reach the pretty marina area walk on the raised pavement past the Blackwater Marina and Hopper's Bar. Keep on the right of two concrete footpath signs. Join the concrete sea wall to the east.

2. Climb over a stile, admiring Osea Island to your north. Follow along the wall, making north-east along Mundon Creek and north to pass alongside Lawling Creek. As Cannery House comes into view to the east (it is a large development including caravans on the other side of

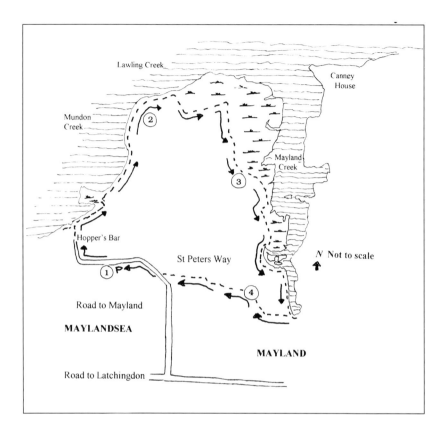

Mayland Creek) the path turns right and you pick up sight of Steeple church to the east.

3. Walk to the south with saltings on your left, gradually approaching the waterside. Keep walking south over three stiles. Just past a yellow arrow turn right going westward up a broad tree-lined path. You have now joined the St Peter's Way. At the end of the path turn right and pass to the left of Anglian Water.

4. Continue downhill with old market garden buildings on the left till you come to a stream. A stile and bridge enable you to cross the stream. Continue over a pasture field and cross a fence near a gate. Follow the road to the right, then keep left along the backs of gardens. After 300 yards turn left up the lane to the main road in Mayland. Turn right to reach your car by the shops.

Mayland Creek

PLACES OF INTEREST NEARBY

Northey Island, Maldon, off the B1018 from Latchingdon about 2 miles past Mundon Northey, is next door to Osea Blackwater Estuary and has a large area of undisturbed saltmarsh. Regular open days and visits by appointment with the Warden when times and tides permit. Telephone 01621 853142.

To reach *New Hall Vineyards*, Chelmsford Road, Purleigh, follow the B1012 about 2 miles west from Latchingdon then about 1 mile north to Purleigh. Look for the brown vineyard signs. Cellar shop, vineyard walk, farm walk, tastings. Guided tours of winery available plus open days. Telephone 01621 828343.

WALK 14

HISTORIC MALDON

Maldon is the setting for a walk by river, canal and estuary and this ancient town provides history and picturesque buildings in abundance as well as marvellous views.

Maldon

Beeleigh Weir is a waterways super-highway junction! The Rivers Blackwater and Chelmer, the Chelmer and Blackwater Navigation and the Langford Cut all join and separate here, so you can expect a delightful network of bridges, weirs and waterways. As you walk towards the weir you will already have had views of historic Northey Island, where a Viking raiding party camped before crossing the causeway and defeating the English in AD 991, and across the River Chelmer to Heybridge. You can watch the working boats as you make your way towards the fine new bridge over the navigation. The Maldon Crystal Salt Company is a reminder that once salt pans would have been common along the coast, though today it is the only company still

66

producing crystal salt for the table by evaporation. Maldon is indeed an old and fascinating town, with so much to see that you may wish to call in at the Tourist Information Centre and pick up some leaflets to make sure you don't miss anything. The walk route will take you past the 15th-century Moot Hall and the even older Blue Boar inn, outside where the medieval fish market was held, and to two lovely and ancient churches – All Saints with its unique 13th-century triangular tower, and St Mary's whose tower was once an important marker for seafarers.

Maldon is crammed with eating places to suit all tastes. Wheelers Fish Bar at the top of the High Street is a must for those liking well cooked fish and chips. You can get wine or lager here as well as tea and coffee to accompany your meal. Telephone 01621 853647 to book a table. Just round the corner you will find the Blue Boar a fine old inn. They will be able to provide you with a good meal or a room if you want to stay. Telephone 01621 852681. Further down the High Street is the much smaller but very reasonably priced Rose and Crown. Look on the board outside to get a feel for the value for money dishes they offer. Telephone 01621 854175. I have just scratched the surface of the eating and drinking possibilities in Maldon. You can further choose between two good Chinese houses, three curry houses, a bistro, many take-aways and pubs and Val's fresh sea food shed. I would strongly advise you make this trip one where you have time to try at least one of the temptations on offer!

- **HOW TO GET THERE:** From the south take the A414 to Maldon from the A12. From the north leave the A12 at Hatfield Peverel on the B1019. Make your way into Maldon via the bypass going anti-clockwise. The way is marked 'B1018 Burnham', then you will see the brown signs for the Leisure Centre and Promenade Park, which is right next to the entrance to the Civic Amenity and re-cycling site.
- **PARKING:** You can park for free on Park Drive, but preferably turn right into the park heading for the far right-hand corner. The charge here is £1 for 3 hours, just time to do the walk and have a meal. Free parking is also available at point 6 in the lay-by on the bypass, and you could then follow the walk from there.
- **LENGTH OF THE WALK:** 4½ miles. Map: OS Landranger 168 Colchester and The Blackwater (GR 862064).

THE WALK

1. Make your way to the right-hand corner of Promenade Park. Walk

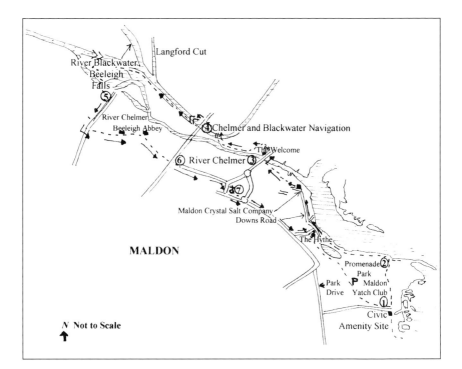

down the steps and come up again by Maldon Yacht Club Road near the civic amenity site. There are good views over to Northey Island here. Turn left along the road till you reach the yacht club then make your way round the railings keeping them on your right. When you reach the pond go over on the road to the groyne.

2. Turn right if you want to look at the view for a while, otherwise turn left and walk into Maldon along the promenade. Go to the right of the swimming pool. On a hot day you may wish to join the bathers for a swim, it's free! Pass Hythe Quay, the Queen's Head pub and Maldon Chandlery and then go half-left into Downs Road. The views over the river here are superb. You can take the lower path through the park if you wish. The playgroup will appear on your left. Continue ahead into the private road that takes you past the Maldon Crystal Salt Company, one of the last remaining salt pans in England. Go ahead through Bath Place Wharf then keep left of the green railings, walk on behind the craft workshops and down to the road.

68

Beeleigh Abbey

3. Turn right to cross the Chelmer bridge and then cross the road with care. Take the footpath left at the rear of The Welcome, marked 11. Go down the twitten to exit by Maldon Royal Mail. Cross the road and take the footpath sign left up the steps to the sea wall. Turn right and walk the sea wall to the end of the store car park. Leave the sea wall to cross the new bridge over the canal.

4. Follow the path right and right again to take you under the bridge you just crossed and under the bridge ahead. Up a small slope you will see a metal lock bridge. Cross to the other side of the Chelmer and Blackwater Navigation. Turn right to walk along the banks till you pass a golf club on your left. Watch for any golf balls! You soon reach the red brick bridge and lock, the start of the weir complex. Walk on to cross the first wooden bridge above the weir. Just before the next lock turn left and walk through a gate to a further weir bridge with a Maldon Millennium Way sign.

5. Turn left again to cross the bridge. Continue ahead to a metal gate and the road. Turn right and follow this for ½ mile. At the road junction turn left by a footpath sign to pass Beeleigh Abbey, now the home of the Foyle family. Continue ahead to cross a stile with a waymark. The path goes slightly right to a second stile, over this you find yourself on an uphill hedged path. Follow this to a roadside stile.

6. Cross the bypass with care and climb up the long flight of stairs to a stile. Over this the route, still uphill, takes you suddenly to a wide unmade road. Look for the fenced twitten ahead, this leads you onto Beeleigh Road. Walk the length of this then cross into Silver Street.

7. Opposite the Blue Boar turn left into Church Walk. Glimpse left to see the old vicarage as you go right through the churchyard. Pass Spindles on your way to the High Street. If you have time, a visit to All Saints church with its triangular tower is well worth it. Turn left and stop under the red bricked Moot Hall entrance – you may want to visit the famous Maldon Embroidery or just read the roll call of historic sites in the town listed here. Continue down the High Street till you can turn left into Church Street. Then turn right to St Mary's church. Take the path to the right of the church to an iron gate, then walk right a few steps up the lane and then left back through the metal gate into Promenade Park. You can now make your own way back by the direct route to your car, or perhaps stop off for some of Val's sea food down by the marina pool or visit one of the other distractions. The choice is yours!

PLACES OF INTEREST NEARBY

The Marine Centre, Hythe Quay has displays on the history of the port of Maldon. Telephone 01621 852290 for opening times. *Promenade Park* has an adventure playground, picnic sites, amusements, tennis courts and mini golf, pedalos on the lake and boat trips on the river plus a programme of events in the park from April to September. More details from the tourist office. Telephone 01621 856503.

WALK 15

BLACKWATER BY THE SEA

Some of the finest views in Essex (bring your binoculars!) enhance this walk on the Blackwater estuary at Heybridge where a river and a canal meet.

Heybridge Basin

The Blackwater estuary is the widest section of salt water contained in the county of Essex and the inland rivers leading to it are among the most complicated. First, there are two rivers both flowing through Essex, the Chelmer and the Blackwater. The Chelmer rises to the east of Debden and curiously the Blackwater rises not so far away by Saffron Walden, though it goes under the ancient name of Pant as far as Braintree. I sometimes feel sorry for the Chelmer. It flows all these miles gathering two significant tributaries (the Wid and the Can) and when just within a few yards of the sea it is joined by the Blackwater. On the strength of this river being a little bit longer, the estuary is called the Blackwater. A further complication is the Chelmer and

71

Blackwater Canal. In this case the canal follows the course of the Chelmer from Chelmsford. At Beeleigh Weirs the river goes its own way and the canal jumps in with the nearby Blackwater. Again this river flows to Heybridge and joins the Chelmer at Heybridge Creek. Just before this the canal departs on the last mile to Heybridge Basin and the sea by the lock. It is by the splendid routes of the canal and river that our walk is sited. We start near the lock at Heybridge Basin and passing later by the Heybridge parish church. Over the water St Mary's church is a landmark for river craft coming up the Blackwater. The views over the salt marshes near the river are some of the finest in Essex. The walk is rich in bird life so you may wish to bring your binoculars along today.

Food and drink are available at the start or end of the walk at the Jolly Sailor at Heybridge. This old pub is situated very close to the sea wall and the lock. Customers are welcomed with good beer and a range of excellent hot meals. The meat pie I had on my last visit was delicious. Telephone 01621 854210. Around Heybridge church a number of pubs are close by. If the time is right Copsey's fish restaurant is equally close.

- HOW TO GET THERE: From Chelmsford the A414 through Danbury and the northern Maldon bypass leads to the causeway at Heybridge. From here follow the signs towards Goldhanger and turn right signposted to Heybridge Basin.
- PARKING: As you enter the heart of Heybridge Basin turn off right signposted as a free car park. For easy access to the canal wall park well into the area.
- LENGTH OF THE WALK: 3¼ miles. Map: OS Landranger 168 Colchester and the Blackwater (GR 871068).

THE WALK

1. From the fine large car park in Heybridge Basin climb up on to the wall of the canal where many yachts are berthed. Turn right along the canal. Here the waters are quiet but when commercial traffic was frequent years ago there were many barges sailing up and down to Chelmsford. The journey from here to Heybridge is about a mile and passes the rather sad remains of Heybridge Hall which sustained a fire in recent years. Fear not, there is a restoration proceeding.

2. You come to a road bridge dated 1910 built by the Essex County Council. Climb up to the road and turn left crossing the bridge. You are in the centre of Heybridge. The church is beyond on the right but the

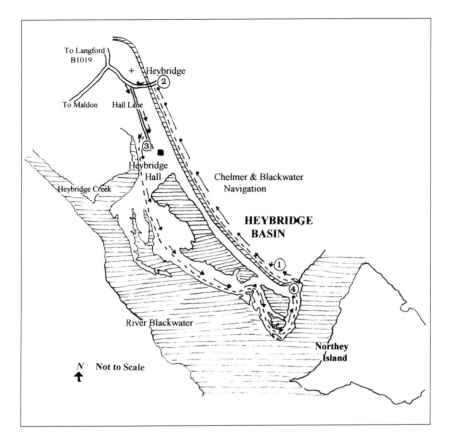

road curves to the right and faces Copsey's Fish Restaurant. Turn left along Hall Road.

3. Now follow a sign announcing 'Footpath on sea wall'. This is the River Blackwater which shortly goes into Heybridge Creek on its way to join the Chelmer on its journey to the sea. Your sea wall route stays on its elevated path and passes the broad river on the right and a deep inland lake produced by several gravel pits on your left. The path sweeps to the left and then sharply to your left heading north past Northey Island to reach the lock at Heybridge Basin.

4. Cross the lock and you are confronted with the difficult choice between the food and drink on offer at the Old Ship or the Jolly Sailor.

A view of Maldon from the riverbank

PLACES OF INTEREST NEARBY

A trip to *Maldon* is an opportunity to take a wander up the historic High Street. The Moot Hall contains a tapestry produced for the Maldon Millennium a few years ago, and outside the hall are listed several other old buildings to be seen. Telephone 01621 857373.

TOLLESBURY AND OLD HALL MARSHES

Birdwatching has replaced smuggling as the main activity on Old Hall Marshes near Tollesbury and this is a fascinating walk along the sea wall and back to an historic little town with an interesting church.

Tollesbury Fleet

Tollesbury has a very mature look with many quaint old buildings in the central streets. On Church Street the proportions are just right and the green has become a paved square with the church at one end and the King's Head at the other. The square is dominated by the massive church tower which rests on the oldest stones the village has. Indoors, above the 14th-century tower arch, is a course of Roman tiles the Saxon builders used. A Norman window close by has a representation of St Cedd the Saxon bishop. The small font may pass unnoticed, yet it

75

has an odd little story. It was obtained for the church in 1718 by a strong-willed churchwarden from John Norman, who came into the church cursing during service. To prevent his being prosecuted he paid five pounds, and out of this sum the font was bought. Round the bowl was inscribed: 'Good people all I pray take care, That in the church you do not swear, As this man did'. In more prosperous trading times there was a branch line of the railway which connected Tollesbury and Witham. This has been succeeded by an air of peace and quiet which is most attractive for all that. To the north of the little town are situated Old Hall Marsh and Salcott Channel. We believe that hereabouts was a veritable haven for smuggling. Now the marshes are owned by the Royal Society for the Protection of Birds, an altogether more laudable activity.

The King's Head on the square once had a sombre look and its viability could have been in doubt. Now with a younger landlord at the helm it seems that good times are ahead. The interior is smart with lots of ancient beams exposed, and the food is all very acceptable. Oh yes, the beer is good too! Telephone 01621 869203. The Hope Inn along the High Street is of rather more modern construction (70 years old) and here also you can rely on the food being wholesome, matching the drinks. Telephone 01621 869238.

- **HOW TO GET THERE:** Almost midway between Maldon and Colchester make for Tolleshunt d'Arcy on the B1026. Now take the B1023 road signposted to Tollesbury which is not much more than a mile distant.
- **PARKING:** You should find space in Church Street by the King's Head.
- **LENGTH OF THE WALK:** 5¾ miles. Map: OS Landranger 168 Colchester and the Blackwater (GR 956104).

THE WALK

1. From Church Street turn right along East Street and soon left along Woodrolfe Road to the Marina. There are several interesting features here including craft shops and boatbuilding and repairing enterprises.

2. Turn left when you see a concrete public footpath sign joining the sea wall. Soon you will reach the re-routed wall which is an experiment to give back to the sea a section of land. Later you rejoin the old wall leading to Old Hall Farm.

3. Just beyond the cottages climb down from the wall and turn right

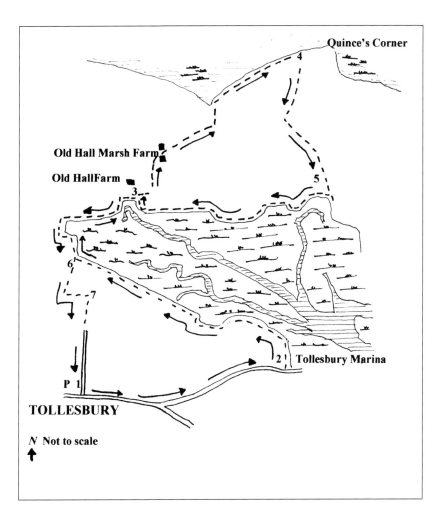

along the farm road. When you see a sign leading to the offices turn left and follow this cutting through the farm steading to cross a stile. Pass over a pasture land for sheep and reach another stile. Now turn left and climb onto the sea wall.

4. Soon you will come to another stile just before Quince's Corner and a track marked 'short cut'. This is the ancient track you take right across the marshes to the sea wall on the south.

5. Here you cross another stile. The path on this side is more

77

The marina at Tollesbury

overgrown but you can spot the Tollesbury Marina in the distance as well as Bradwell power station and probably St Peter's Chapel. Ignore some steps down on your right and on reaching Old Hall Farm keep up on the wall. Past the farm turn left and at the next corner when you see a track off to the right leave the wall.

6. Immediately turn left (south-east) on a field edge path. At the corner turn right for 30 yards then left through a gap in the hedge on a hedged path leading to a paved track by a concrete public footpath sign.

7. Turn right and this leads you eventually to Station Road and the town centre. All the town streets are full of interest with houses mainly from 60 to 150 years old.

PLACES OF INTEREST NEARBY

Maldon and District Agricultural and Domestic Museum is at 47 Church Street, Goldhanger. Open Sunday and Wednesday only. Telephone 01621 788647 for more information.

FORD STREET AND THE RIVER COLNE

The River Colne meandering towards Colchester has been crossed for centuries at Ford Street, the start of a lovely walk along the river and across an ancient water meadow, with views across the valley.

A footbridge over the River Colne

Ford Street is a group of fine old houses around the banks of the River Colne - no church, no school but three pubs, suggesting a stopping point for those coming from north or south to cross the river. It is understood that formerly the road did not cross the river other than by a ford. Part of the walk follows the river and crosses south on a footbridge which was only put in place in 1996 after lengthy appeals by the ramblers locally. The route also crosses an ancient water meadow, then climbs to 100 feet, which height affords lovely views to the north over Fordham church and beyond. On the south side of the river Ford Street is part of Aldham parish. On the other side it is within Fordham parish.

Three excellent pubs offer themselves for your nourishment. The

Coopers Arms and the Queen's Head are on the south side of the river. The Coopers Arms provides solid pub fare and always has coffee available. Telephone 01206 241177. The Queen's Head has good cuisine, an interesting selection of ornaments and a restaurant separated from the main bar. The car park has an ordered in and out arrangement to cope with the somewhat narrow entrance. Telephone 01206 241291. Over the bridge the Shoulder of Mutton, a long time favourite of ours, provides the selection you may enjoy for regular eating and drinking. Telephone 01206 240464.

- **HOW TO GET THERE:** Ford Street is on the A604, a few miles west of the A12 interchange.
- **PARKING:** You may park on the road, or perhaps in one of the pub car parks if you first seek the landlord's permission.
- **LENGTH OF THE WALK:** 2½ miles. Map: OS Landranger 168 Colchester and the Blackwater (GR 920270).

THE WALK

1. Go north over the river from your parking place. Turn right through the grounds of the Shoulder of Mutton with the river Colne close on your right to reach an arable field. Turn right along the field edge following the river.

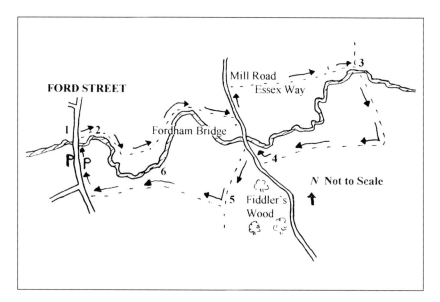

Ford Street from the river bridge

2. When the river bears right a path goes left through the field. Follow this to rejoin the river. The path now continues east to the road by the concrete footpath sign. Turn left and cross the road to a second concrete footpath post. Walk to the right of a back garden and pick up the path (the Essex Way) continuing east. You shortly join the river bank. After 400 yards you come to a wooden bridge crossing the Colne.

3. Cross the bridge into the water meadow, you will often find sheep grazing hereabouts. Make your way south uphill. About 100 yards to your right there is a wide gap between two old hedges. Turn right and walk through this gap. Your direction is now towards the road and to spot the stile ahead and walk to it.

4. Turn right (north) and walk down the road. Just before the road bridge over the river turn left at a concrete footpath post and follow the cross-field path south uphill with Fiddler's Wood on your left.

5. When you come to a yellow arrow pointing right turn right, but first pause to admire the views to the north. Follow the path round the field edge to cross a plank at the field corner.

6. Through the hedge follow the river. You will be able to survey across the river the route you took on your outward journey from this point. When the river turns right continue straight on for 50 yards to the road by a stile and footpath sign. Turn right into Ford Street and back to your car.

PLACES OF INTEREST NEARBY

Just on the edge of Ford Street in New Road is *Mill Race Nursery*. It is well worth a visit for its fine selection of plants, dried and silk flowers, garden ornaments etc. There is a grassed area right beside the river and the Essex Way crosses the nursery on its way into the village. There are boats to be hired so you can take a row round on the river Colne and a small cafeteria caters for teas and snack lunches. Admission free, open 9 am to 5.30 pm. For more information telephone 01206 242521.

CHAPPEL AND THE COLNE VALLEY
✿❧✿

A magnificent 19th-century railway viaduct crosses the Colne Valley near Chappel. A pretty village, the peaceful River Colne and some lovely countryside combine to make this a very special walk.

The start of the walk

The Colne Valley between Halstead and Fordham is in a tranquil part of Essex and contains some of the most satisfying pastoral countryside to be found in this county. Chappel, a small hamlet near Wakes Colne, is dominated by a large railway viaduct of 1847 crossing the valley, 100 feet high and containing 30 arches. It is used by the nearby East Anglian Railway Museum who run the occasional train over it. However, Chappel can be much admired on its own merits. Next to the church is a handsome little Georgian house with plaster panels. Above the roof of the church rises a wooden belfry with a short spire, and the ancient door leads us to a nave with 14th-century walls. The walk starts in the middle of Chappel by the church and then follows the river upstream to a newly fashioned fishing lake before turning south for excellent views. Soon we join the Essex Way downhill back to join the river and head for the viaduct, going under this to regain the village.

The pub in the village is the Swan dated 1390. It has customers from far and wide and can cater with its extensive menu for all tastes. There is an excellent courtyard dining area where children are allowed to sit and eat. It is situated by the river, and is well worth a visit. Telephone 01787 222353.

- **HOW TO GET THERE:** Chappel lies on the A604 between Halstead and the A12 to Colchester. It is just to the west of the viaduct.
- **PARKING:** There is a village car park past the Swan on the left near the church.
- **LENGTH OF THE WALK:** 3¼ miles. Map: OS Landranger 168 Colchester and the Blackwater (GR 895284).

THE WALK

1. From the car park walk past the church and straight on past the barn. You are following the course of the River Colne which is 100 yards or so to the right with an attractive mill just beyond. Cross a stile and bear left. Cross another stile and turn to the right. Follow a yellow arrow with a hedge on your right and go over two more stiles and a plank bridge. (This is a stylish walk, isn't it?) Go over another stile into a meadow with a fishing lake. In the corner of the meadow and the wood ahead cross a rather makeshift stile which leads to a smarter stile with arrows and waymarks.

2. At the end of the wood on your left turn left over a stile with waymarks and walk uphill along the path in the woods for ½ mile till you reach Priory House. Keep to the left of the hedge past the house and follow the metalled drive, swinging left to the road at a concrete public footpath sign.

3. Cross the road just to the left and at another public footpath sign turn right up some steps to a field. Head across the field aiming for two thatched roofs. Walk along Bacons Lane through Swan Street.

4. At a concrete public footpath sign turn right past houses with a hedge on your right. After 150 yards go through a gap in the corner of the field to find a yellow arrow and pass a pond on your right. Follow

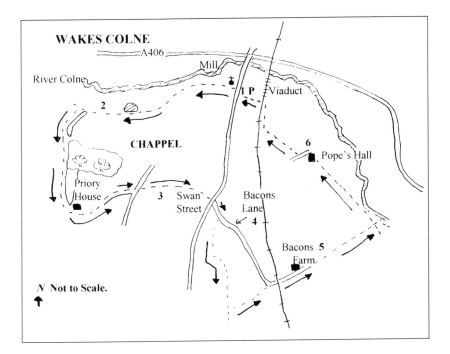

the field edge to the corner and turn left past the hedge with an Essex Way sign. Join the farm drive on a corner and continue over the railway to Bacons Farm. At the back of the buildings there are two paths.

5. Turn left with the Essex Way sign and walk downhill towards the river. You will be able to enjoy a fine view here of the valley, the viaduct and the country scene. Just before the river bridge and gate turn left over two stiles, aiming to the right of Pope's Hall ahead. Follow past the Hall, and turn left onto the lane.

6. Soon turn right across a field towards the viaduct. Join a path to the right beside and below the railway. On reaching the viaduct cross through the arches and over a little playing field back to your car.

PLACES OF INTEREST NEARBY
The East Anglian Railway Museum is at Chappel & Wakes Colne Station, Wakes Colne. A working museum housing rolling stock, steam and diesel locomotives, signal box and station. Cafe and picnic area. Open 10 am to 5 pm. Telephone 01206 242524.

ST OSYTH AND POINT CLEAR
᠊ᥫᦞᥛ᠊

On this superb creekside walk with great historic interest, St Osyth's magnificent abbey, a Martello tower and views across the Rivers Colne and Blackwater will make it a day to remember.

St Osyth's Creek

St Osyth was originally known as Chich, an appropriate name for a winding creek. The East Saxon King Sighere founded here a nunnery for the benefit of his Queen Osyth who became the first abbess. It was perilously near the sea and raiding Danes took the Abbess prisoner. When she refused to renounce her faith they beheaded her. The remains of the abbey are substantial, with certainly the most splendid abbey gate in the country. Above the gateway there is a niche with an exquisite canopy, and the spandrels contain figures of St Michael and the Dragon. St Osyth Abbey is at once magnificent and curious. The main impression is medieval, without the controlling functional design which gave a satisfying pattern to the medieval abbey. By the tower is the spectacle of thousands of red bricks crumbling away. They were made by the Romans, handled by the Saxons and built up by the Normans into the great arches which supported the dormitory of the monks. At the time of writing St Osyth's Priory is closed to the public. As in the past, it may be open in the future so please contact Tendring District Council Tourism Office to check on 01255 253221. The village itself has many ancient cottages. Priory Cottage has a projecting hall of the 15th century, one at the crossroads was built in the 16th century and the moated St Clair Hall in the 14th century. St Osyth church with its massive tower is a noble structure of Tudor days and earlier. In the chancel is a surprise which the villagers have called the Fold, altar rails curiously shaped like a horseshoe. There is a memorial to Benjamin Golding who founded Charing Cross Hospital. The route starts from the Priory for a superb creek-side walk, first along St Osyth Creek and then Brightlingsea Creek. The Martello tower you see ahead was built to repel Napoleon and today houses a museum. Round the corner the views are much wider, across the River Colne to Mersea Island and over the River Blackwater to St Peter's Chapel at Bradwell on Sea.

The Tudor Restaurant in Point Clear is a seaside cafe for nourishment on the way. You will find fresh cooked meals here at everyday prices, no beer but large mugs of steaming hot tea and coffee. Telephone 01255 822245. The Matchbox Inn is open all day and sited near Mill Dam Lake close to the end of the walk. Telephone 01255 820318.

- **HOW TO GET THERE:** From the A133 south-east out of Colchester turn right past the grey towers of the University of Essex on the B1027. Drive through Alresford and Thorrington to reach St Osyth.
- **PARKING:** Park on the grass – a courtesy park in front of the Abbey or just across the road in the car park if there is room. There are toilets just here if you need them.
- **LENGTH OF THE WALK:** 6 miles. (You may wish to catch a bus back from Point Clear. These run frequently and there is a bus stop just down the road and round the corner from the Tudor Restaurant.) Map: OS Landranger 168 Colchester and the Blackwater (GR 122156).

THE WALK

1. Cross the road from the car park and turn left and right by a concrete footpath direction post. Walk down the track and through Warren Farm. From the farm walk downhill towards the creek, Mill Dam Lake.

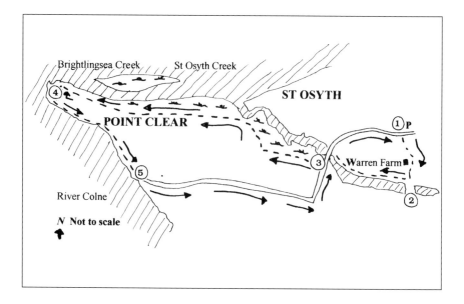

2. Just before the creek turn right through a gap in the hedge and walk along the north bank. At this point the creek has been dammed to form a boating lake. You get superb views across the lake and up the hill beyond. When you reach the road turn left, crossing the creek and the road.

3. At a footpath sign turn right and cross a railed bridge and continue through a kissing gate. Three miles in the distance the towers of Brightlingsea are in sight. The isolation that is St Osyth Creek soon becomes more commercial as the path passes a golf course built not so long ago. Soon you are passing Point Clear on the south, a large holiday complex. You get a close up view over Cinder Island and over to Brightlingsea on the other bank of Brightlingsea Creek. The Martello tower built in 1805 and used by the Navy in the Second World War, guides you nearer to your farthest point along the sea wall.

4. At the path end at the point, turn left, down and along the road for a few yards to spot and follow a concrete footpath sign leading right, back up to the sea wall following south-east. As you turn the corner the Colne estuary comes into view. Follow this good concrete path right along till you come to the Tudor Restaurant. Pass the restaurant on your left and continue uphill for 200 yards to the road.

5. Continue along the road and back over the creek to the Matchbox Inn, a distance of about 2 miles. Along this road you will be fascinated by the range of items offered for sale by the householders and also charmed as we were by the number of double ornaments decorating the front door and fence areas. Those with children will have fun trying to recall the list from dogs to lions and much more.

PLACES OF INTEREST NEARBY

East Essex Aviation Society & Museum at the Martello Tower has First and Second World War displays plus a 'Home Front' display. Admission free. Telephone 01255 428028. It is open Sunday 10 am to 2 pm and other days depending on the time of the year.

Thorrington Tide Mill in Brightlingsea Road, Thorrington is a fully restored 19th-century tide mill with its machinery. Admission free, open last Sunday each month March to September and bank holidays. Telephone 01621 828162.

St Osyth's Priory

THE STOUR ESTUARY AT WRABNESS

❦

*A lovely walk through an RSPB nature reserve and along the Stour
estuary at Wrabness, with wonderful views across into Suffolk and
an unusual belfry to visit.*

The River Stour

Wrabness, on the southern bank of the River Stour, is a very small
village of 300 inhabitants nestling round its railway station. The houses
are a mixture of new and old, and the modern village hall is a credit to
this small community which also boasts its own post office stores. Stour
Estuary Nature Reserve is owned by the Woodland Trust who lease it to
the Royal Society for the Protection of Birds. The walk through the
mainly sweet chestnut trees in Stour Wood brings you to the railway
and across to a large hide overlooking Copperas Bay. After a visit to see
the wading birds and wildfowl your route continues inland on the
banks of the Stour where you have magnificent views over to Holbrook
in Suffolk. You then climb Stone Lane to the ridge and visit All Saints

church to see its most unusual bell cage. This interesting wooden structure houses the church bell, the old church tower having burnt down a couple of centuries ago. The walk back to the village offers excellent views at times right over Harwich and Felixstowe.

Once you have completed your walk the Wheatsheaf (it once traded under the strange name of the Drunken Duck) in Harwich Road offers a warm welcome, a range of beers and an excellent cider. They have a beer garden, restaurant, bar and games room. You will find an extensive choice on their menu which includes bar snacks, sandwiches and the full restaurant menu of a choice of starters, main courses and desserts. They also have a small selection of specials on the blackboard. Telephone 01255 870200.

- **HOW TO GET THERE:** Take the A120T from Colchester towards Harwich and 2 miles after the Wix crossroads turn left. It is signed to Wrabness. Go straight across at the crossroads and just past the station.
- **PARKING:** There is plenty of room to park in Station Road but make sure you do not block anyone's drive. Parking is also available beside the road near (2) on the walk.
- **LENGTH OF THE WALK:** 4 miles. Map: OS Landranger 168 Colchester and the Blackwater (GR 179316).

THE WALK

1. From Station Road, walk back the route you came into the village passing the station, the Old Black Boys pub (now a private house) and the telephone box. Walk on round the corner till you come to the first footpath sign on your left at the corner of the garden of Hill Crest. Walkers from the alternative parking should walk on till they come to this point. Turn left up the gravel drive, you get your first view of Holbrook school across the river. Walk past the farm and turn right at a yellow arrow just before the railway bridge.

2. Your path is just south of east and continues over the field to a stile in the woods ahead. Cross the stile and walk past a RSPB sign. The well marked path takes you round the edge of the woods under sweet chestnut trees. At a crossing gravel track turn right for about 15 feet passing the black metal gate, then turn left to a post and chain gate. Your route continues ahead east on a forest path. When you come to the next junction a path joins from your right and you turn left to pass

91

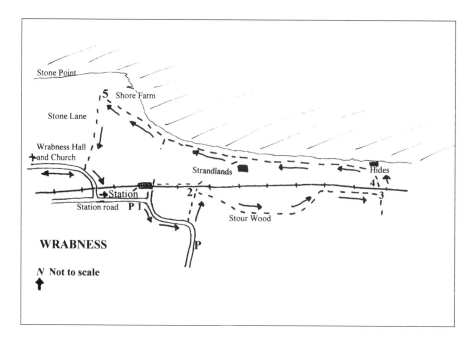

a yellow arrow. After about ¼ mile it turns right, and you cross a stream. Go straight on at a right 'To Car Park' sign, and straight on at the yellow arrow. When you come to the T junction turn left at the sign 'To The Hides' (the right turn here is marked 'To Car Park'). You will be walking north. As another path joins from the left, turn right; the sign reads 'To Hides'. Cross the wooden bridge and climb slightly uphill. Ignore the path to your right and go straight on passing a yellow arrow. Go down four steps and cross the bridge. One further climb with five steps brings you beside the railway line. Walk ahead with the railway on your left and fields on your right till you come to a railway crossing.

3. You need to turn left to cross the railway. An Essex Way sign and yellow arrow and sign 'To Public Hide' all guide you on your way. Across the line take the right-hand path and follow the yellow arrow. This leads downhill to the hide.

4. From the hide retrace your steps and take the path right just above the shore line. Soon the Essex Way and public footpath join from the left. Turn right over the wooden bridge. Another path joins from your left. Turn right to the river bank and go down four steps, over a wooden

The bell cage in the churchyard at Wrabness church

bridge and up the steps to enter a large field. Continue straight ahead to the far corner where you have to cross a stile by Strandlands. You now pass a private hide and have to cross another stile. There is a short cut back to your car by turning left at this point, but you keep straight on along the banks of the River Stour, crossing a bridge and large field till you come to Shore Farm and Stone Lane.

5. At Stone Lane caravan park turn left on the track and walk uphill to the road. Turn right and walk 250 yards to visit All Saints church. You will find the unique bell cage in the churchyard. Retrace your steps to Stone Lane and walk past this on the road. You will pass two seats where you can sit and admire the view. Continue on the road to cross the railway line. Turn left into Station Road and walk past the lovely little village hall on your way back to your car.

PLACES OF INTEREST NEARBY
You are just 5 or 6 miles from *Harwich* so follow the B1352 east. The Harwich Maritime trail guides you through the town, linked to Christopher Jones, the Master of the *Mayflower*, Samuel Pepys, Lord Nelson and Francis Drake. Leaflet available from Harwich Tourist Information Centre, Iconfield Park CO12 4EN. Telephone 01255 506139. Fax 01255 240570.